Art of a

Dragon!

or....

Dan Monroe's

art n' stuff...

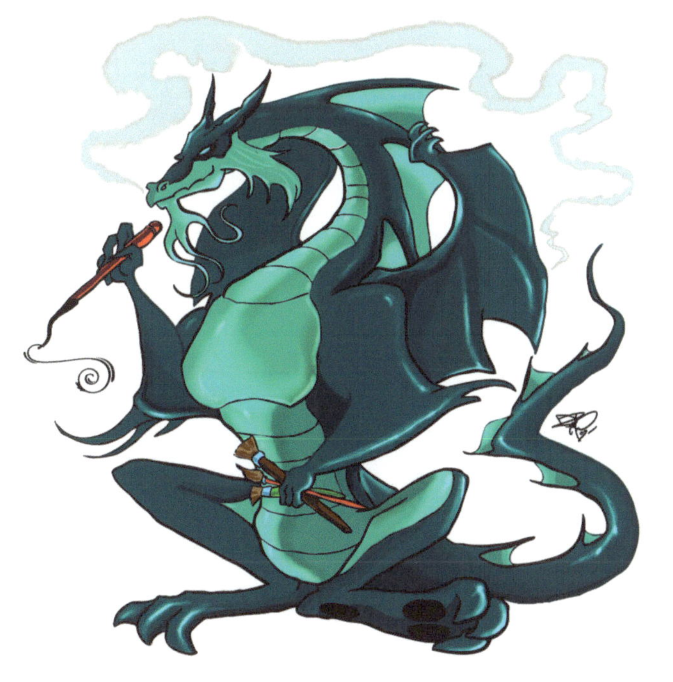

Copyright © 2015

All rights reserved. No part of this book may be reproduced, transmitted,
or stored in any information retrieval system in any form or by any means,
graphic, electronic, or mechanical, including photocopying, taping, and
recording, without prior written permission from the publisher.

Library of Congress Control Number: 2015942437

ISBN-13:
978-0-9960374-7-1

ISBN-10:
0996037470

Art of a Dragon
Volume 1

First edition

Published by:
PencilWerk Press
P.O.Box 452
Paw Paw, Mi 49079

pencilwerkpress.com

Written by,
Character designs, illustrations, cover design. and book design by
Dan Monroe

The veiws expressed within this book are personal opinions of the artist Dan Monroe
aka: Daniel M. Monroe, Dragonbrush, Dragonbrusher.

All artwork and illustrations in this book are the property of Dan Monroe

Printed in the United States of America

For future generations.
Remain true to yourself,
always.

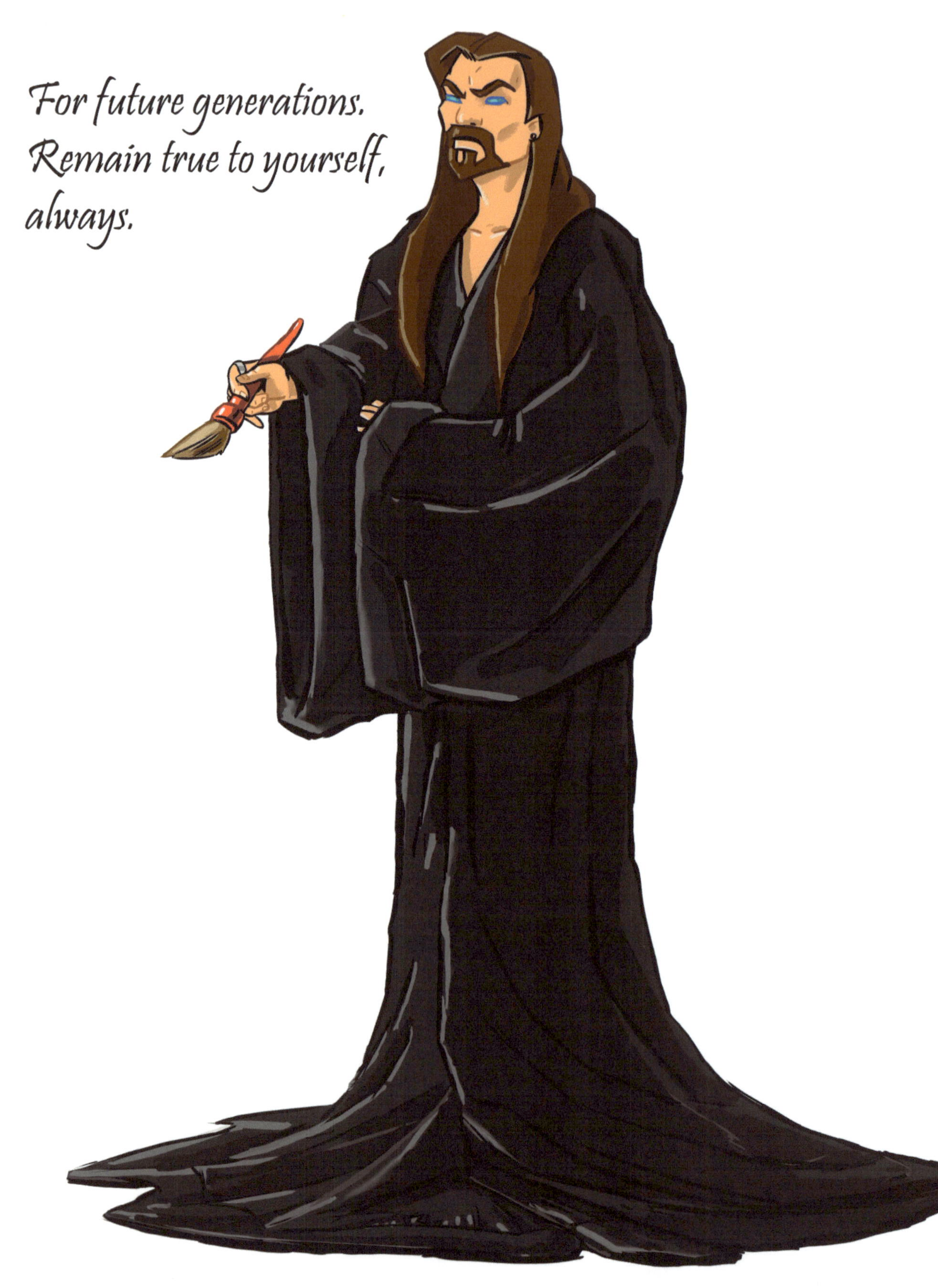

For as long as I can remember, I have been drawing. I have memories of sitting at the dining room table drawing all manner of little monstery things on paper and cutting them out with blunted scissors. On another sheet of paper I would draw backgrounds and play with my little monsters and make up stories and adventures- I was three years old. My love for art and drawing has always been an unquenchable appetite that many have not been able to understand-including my own family members.

Even though I am quite often referred to as a "Children's Illustrator" because everyone feels the need to place us all into a neat category, I have never thought of myself as fitting so neatly into such a niche. My interests are too broad and complicated to label me so simply. Even while putting this book together, and rummaging through pages upon pages of art and sketches to try and figure out the right ones to show, I was hit with the realization of how much I have actually done in my life, the spectrums of my interests, and even the styles that I use to convey the stories that I am trying to tell- or that I have been hired to tell.

I know there are a great many artists in the world who may have more merit than I, and they have no book, while on the other hand, there are a great many whose artistic qualities are far less and they have many books and seem to be loved by the masses. I do hope this book brings some sense of joy and perhaps a bit of artistic inspiration to new artists, whether a novice or a professional. If this book and the illustrations contained within will inspire just one person, well then, I will be very happy indeed.

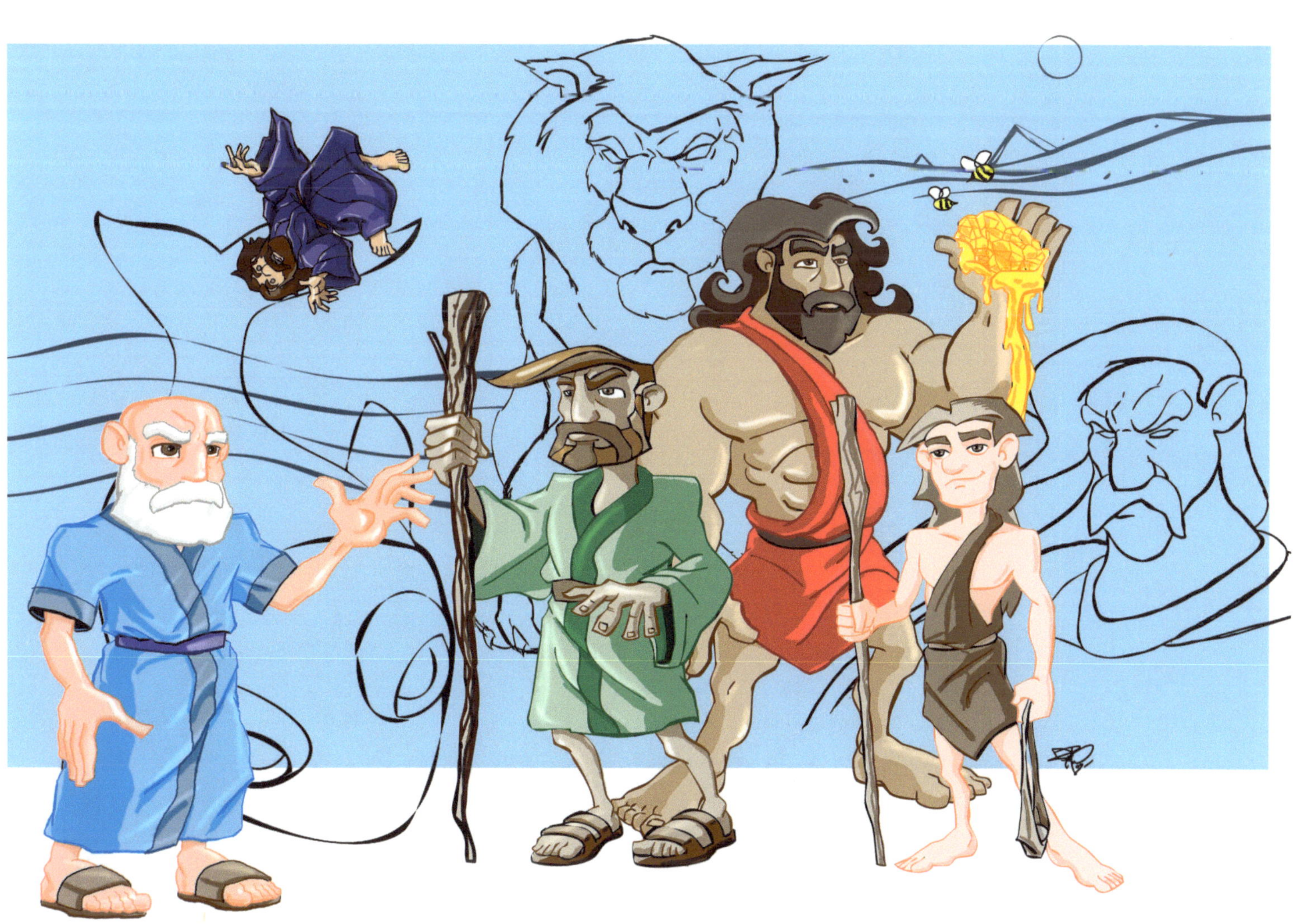

As with all artists-
these characters and drawings
are extensions of me.

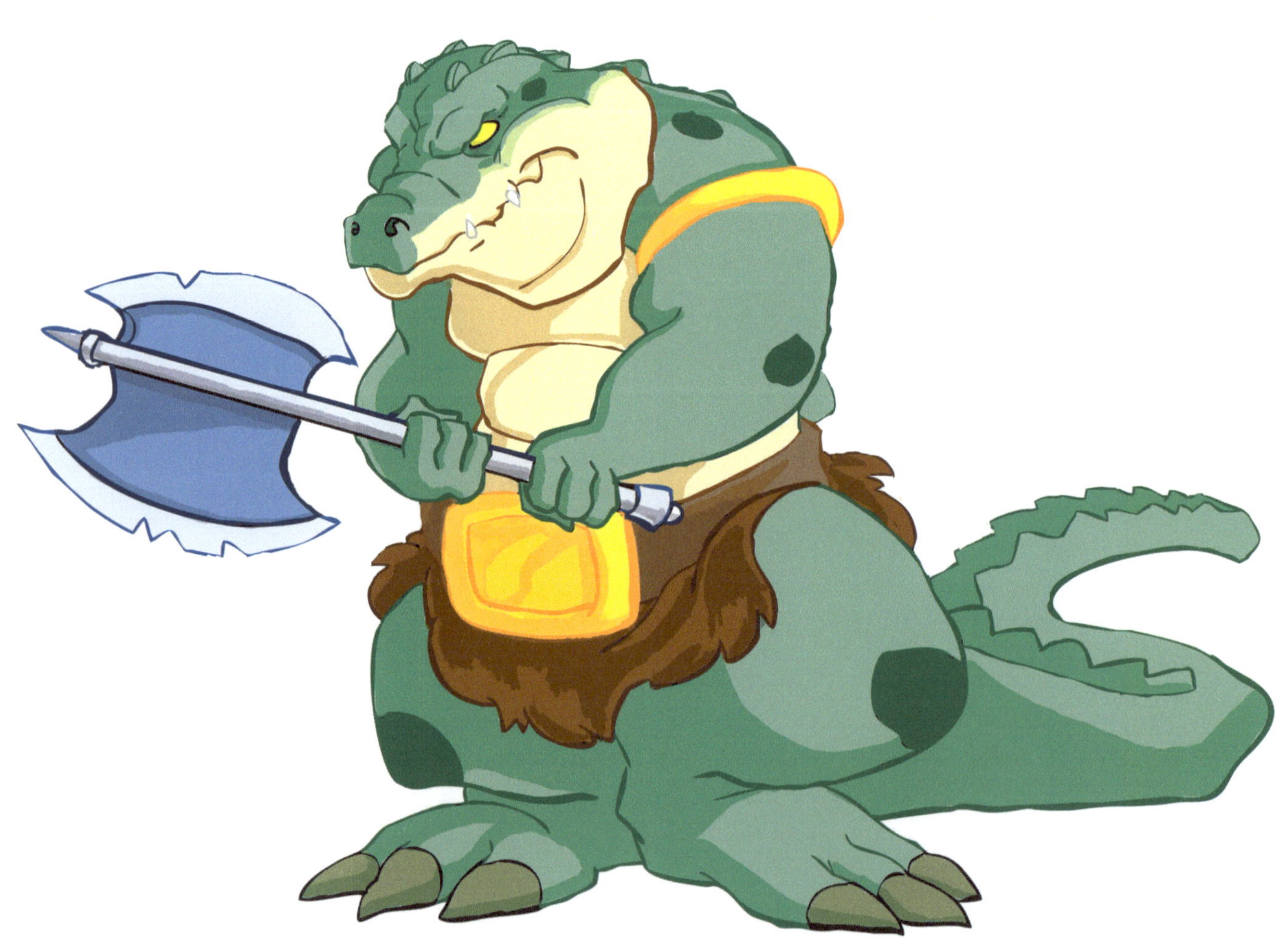

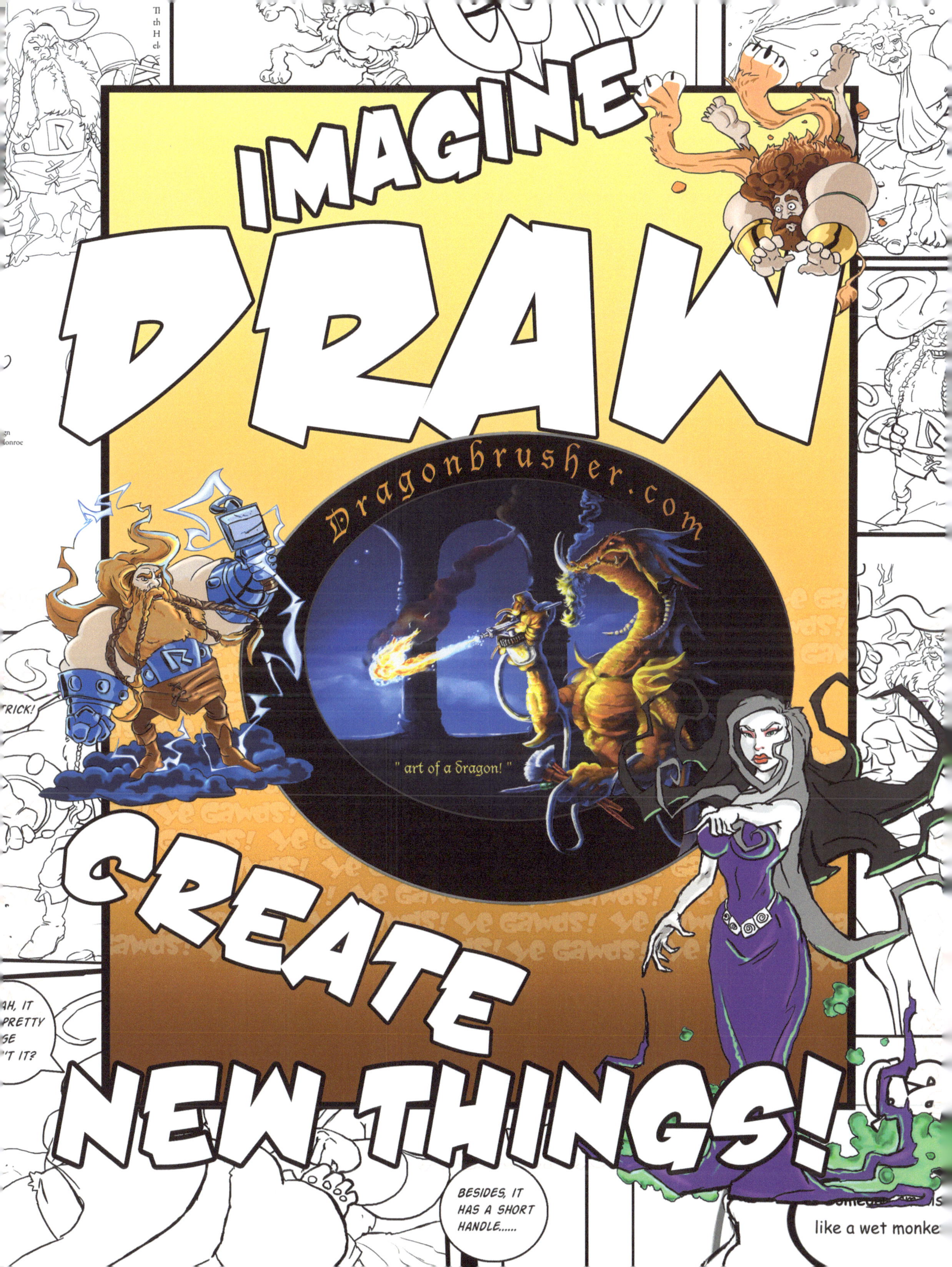

IMAGINE
DRAW
Dragonbrusher.com
" art of a dragon! "
CREATE
NEW THINGS!
TRICK!
AH, IT
PRETTY
GE
'T IT?
BESIDES, IT
HAS A SHORT
HANDLE......
ye Gawds!
like a wet monke

The ways in which I flow...

Actually vary quite a bit. Not only do I produce art in the traditional mediums of pencil, pen, charcoal on paper, paintbrush, and airbrush on canvas - I also do digital art. I firmly believe that as an artist, one must constantly evolve with the times in order to remain current and relevant in an ever-changing landscape. I always produce art in digital medium when I know the end result is for print. It makes it much faster, and cuts out an extra step later on (well, several extra steps, actually), and the publishers appreciate it as well.

I use a Wacom Intuos3 12x12 digital drawing pad when I am working in digital. I find the drawing pad is large enough to accomodate me, and the pressure-sensitive drawing surface is a "must" so that you are able to actually draw on the computer screen with confidence that your "hand" actually remains intact in the art.

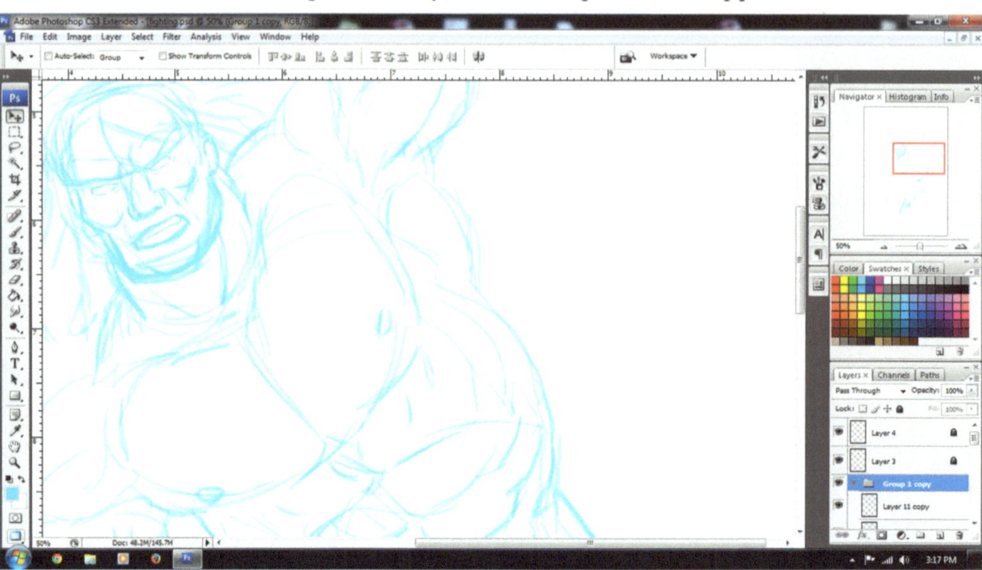

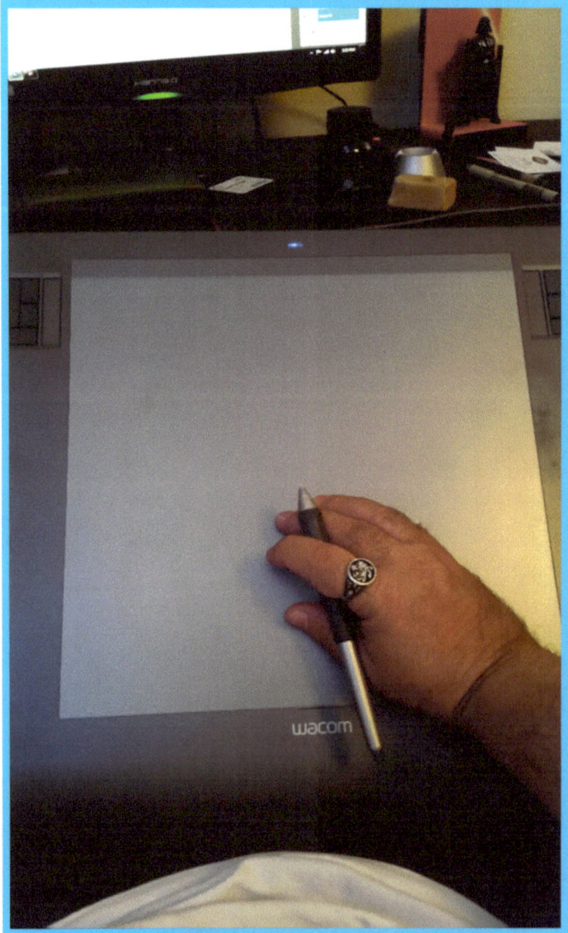

In this photo you can see my Wacom pad as I have it ori-entated upon my lap while I draw in digital. Notice the computer screen on my desktop. I have arranged this page in such a way that, the screenshot above pretty much shows what I see while I am drawing this way.

You will notice there is an eraser, a bottle of ink, and some pens handy, with Darth Vader ever-present and presiding over it all. The traditional tools are always within hands reach for me so that I may switch from digital to traditional materials in an instant when the need arises.

I use a variety of art-producing software when I am working in digital, from Adobe Photoshop CS3, to Painter Classic Pro. It just depends on the project and the style of art that I need or want to produce for it. The different programs all have their pros and cons, quirks and drawbacks, so, over the years I have used them all enough to have developed my own reasonings for using the specific software for the look and feel of the art. Just think, about 8 years ago I was strictly a traditional artist!

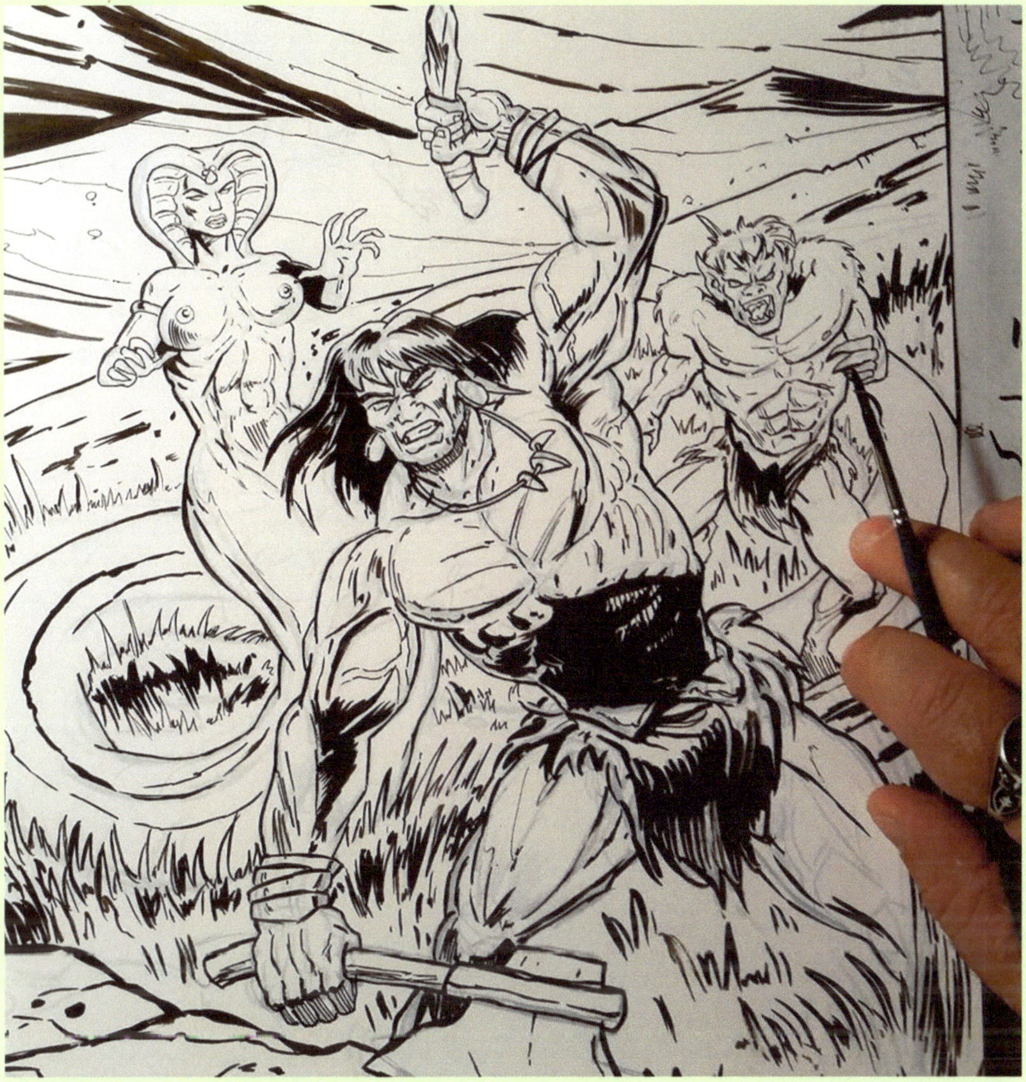

Whether I begin the sketch by digital or traditional means, I always do the inkwork traditionally with brush and nibs. I will also use pens like mocrons, or Faber-Castells.

I prefer using brush and ink, however. The ink quality is just so much better!

This way, I also have a finished ink piece that I can sell, since the sketch of this particular illustration was done digitally. The colors are done in digital as well. This makes for a great work flow!

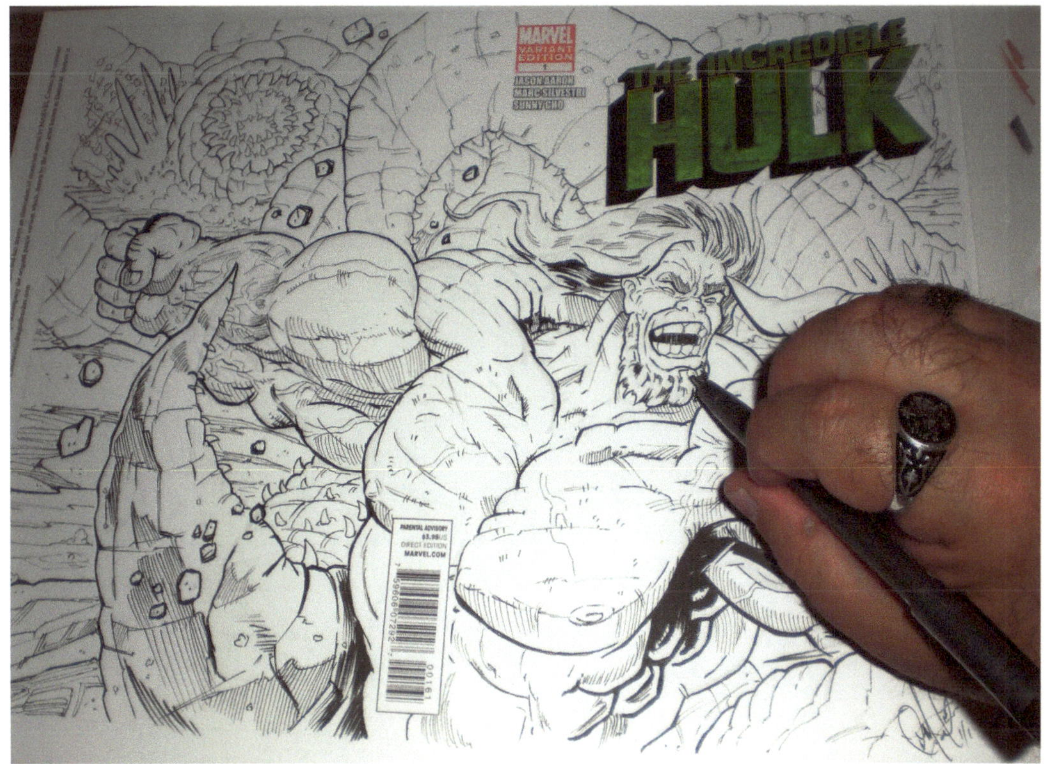

This illustration was sketched on paper, then I scanned the sketch into the computer. I then made the opacity of the lines very light and printed it onto 11X17" bristol.

This makes for a very clean way to ink over my own pencil sketch, and preserves the sketch for sale later on.

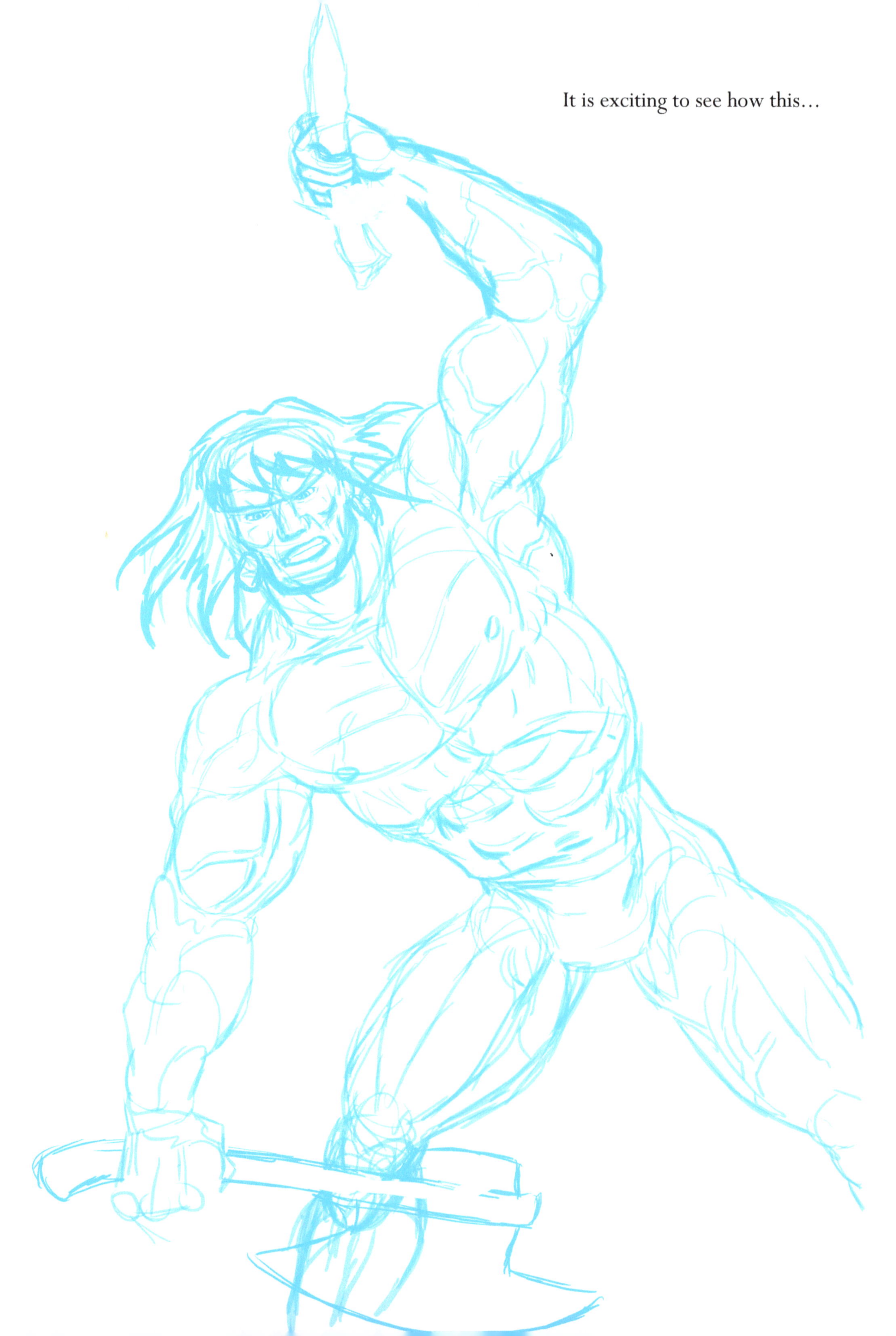

It is exciting to see how this…

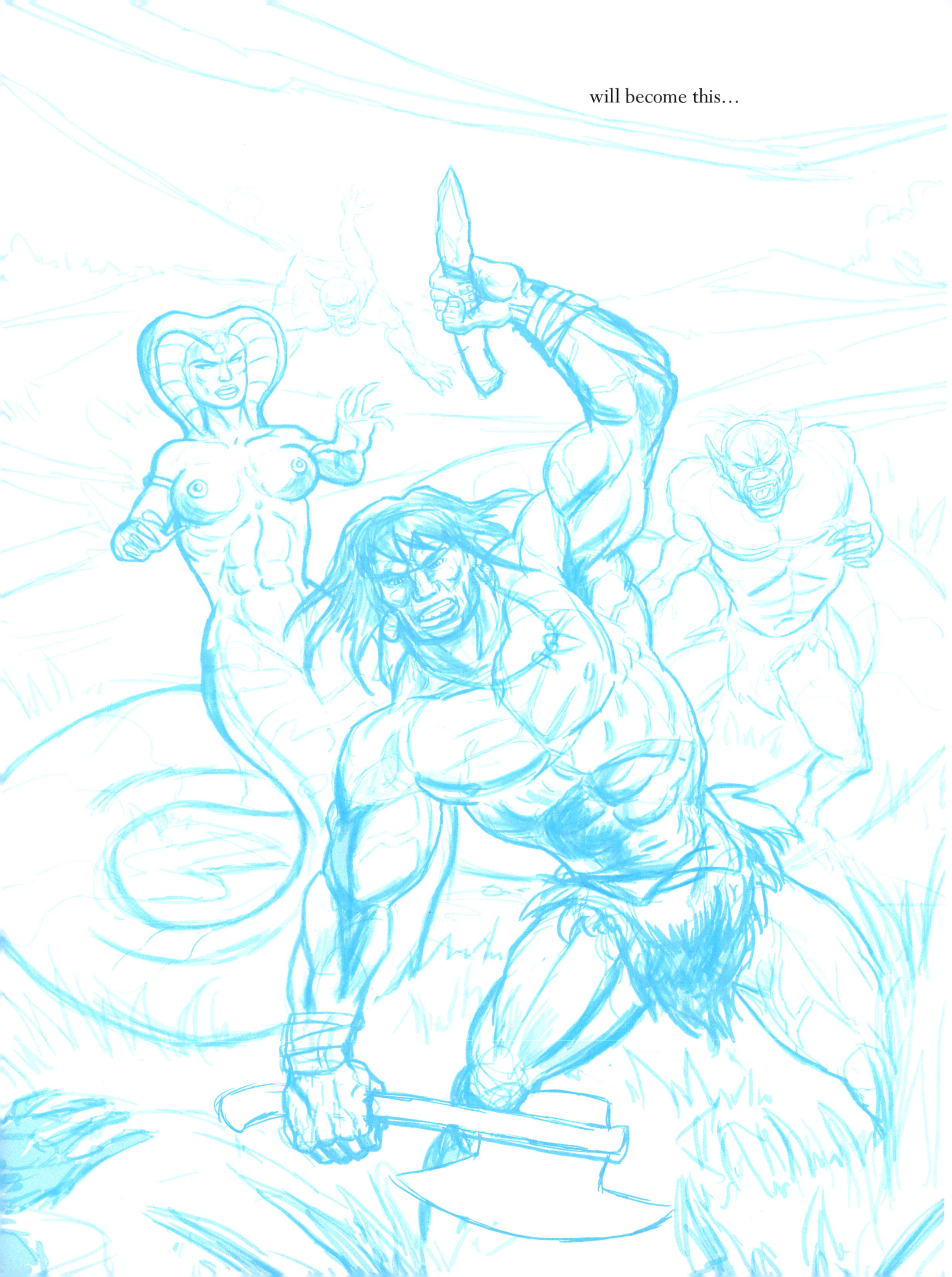
will become this…

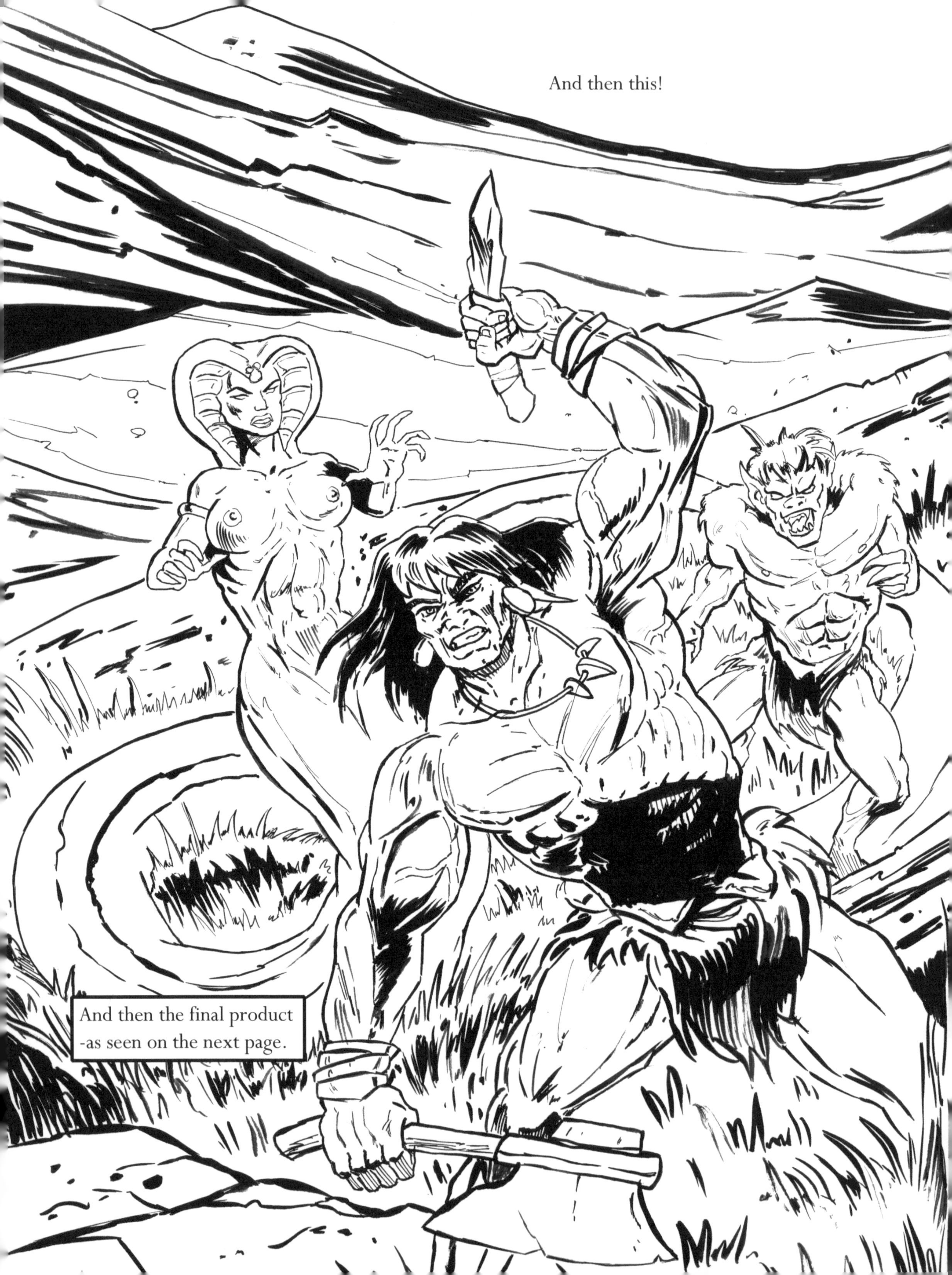
And then this!
And then the final product -as seen on the next page.

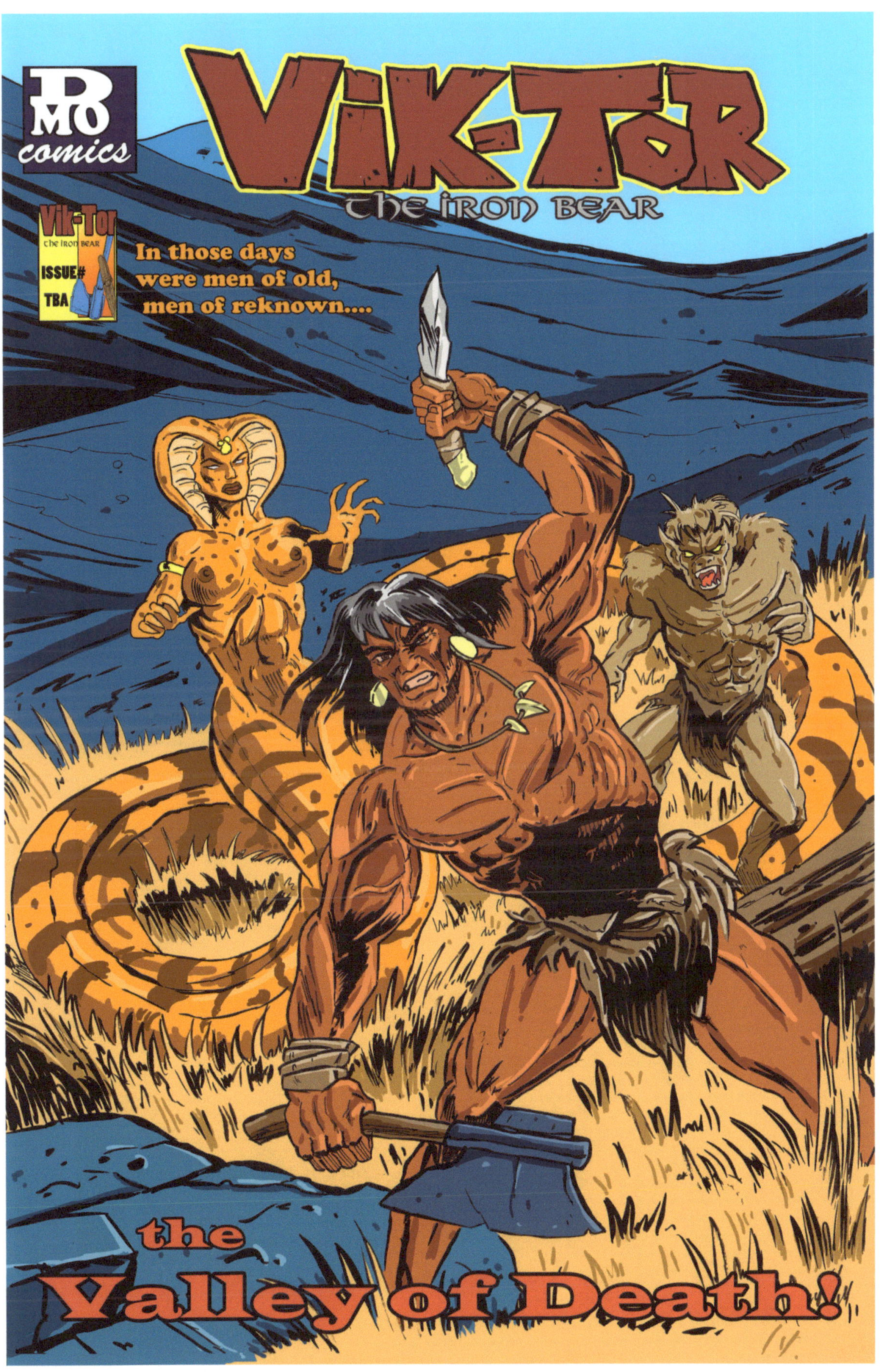

PMO comics
VIK-TOR
THE IRON BEAR
Vik-Tor
the iron bear
ISSUE#
TBA
In those days were men of old, men of reknown....
the Valley of Death!

I draw a great variety of things every day. Some things are not so great, while others are. Some of the not so great drawings however will get under your skin and take on a life of their own!

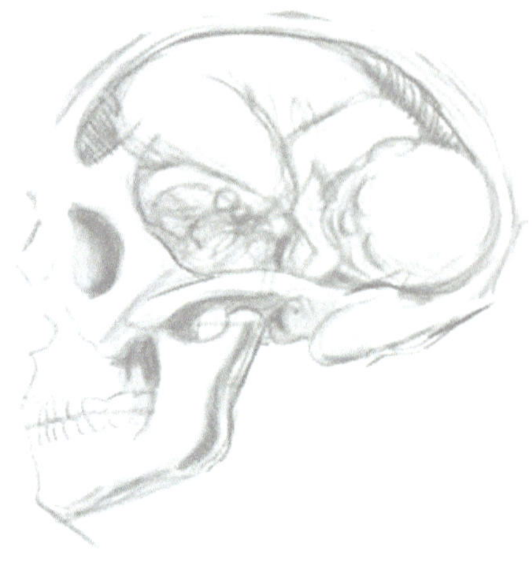

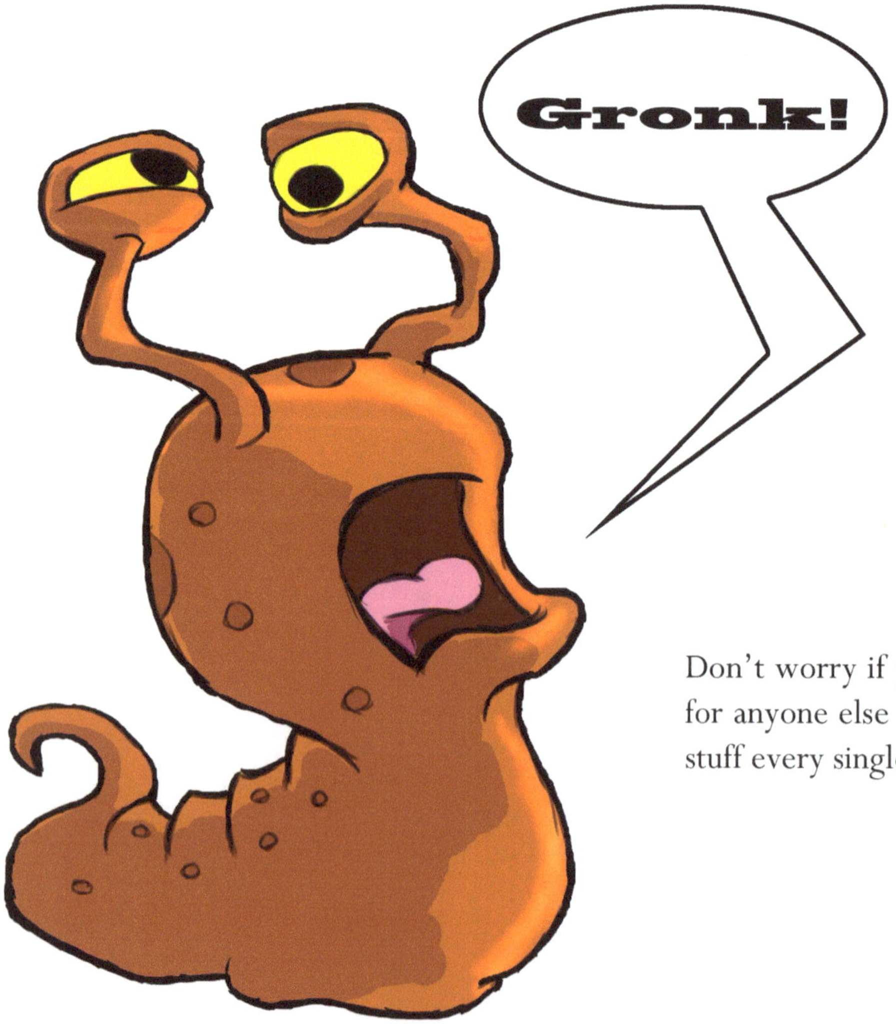

Don't worry if you think it's not good enough for anyone else to see. Just draw stuff. Draw stuff every single day!

Sketches

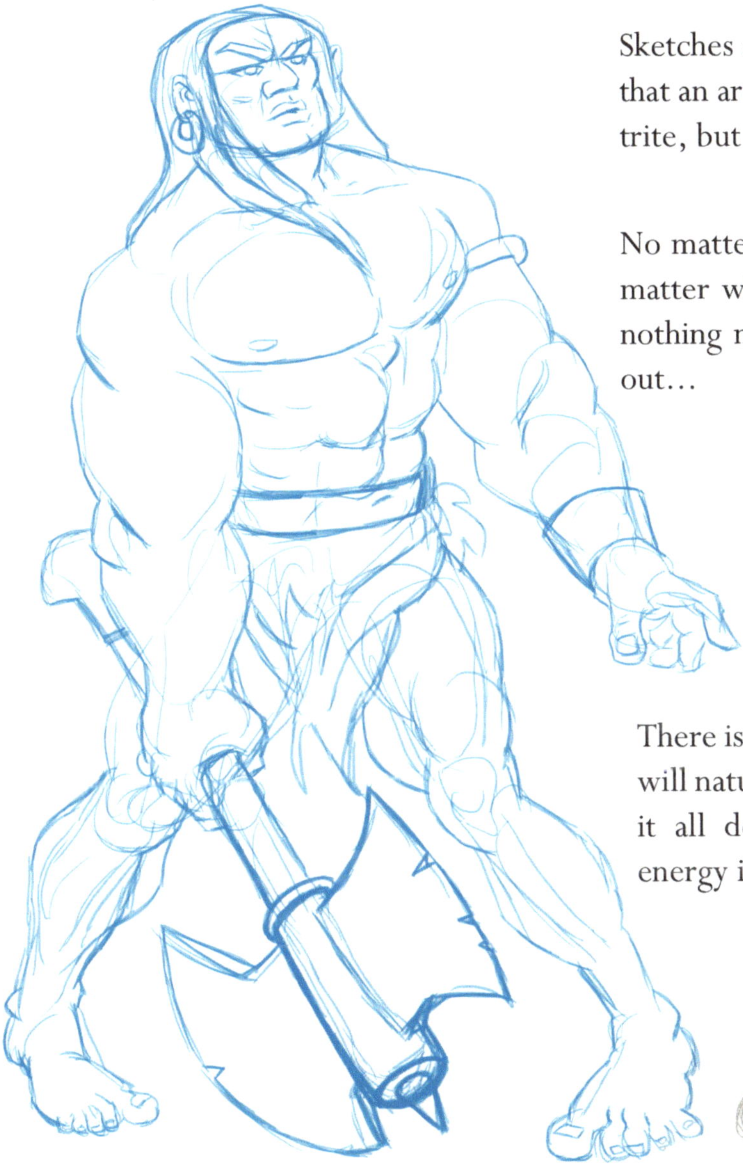

Sketches and sketching are the most important things that an artist should do every single day. It may sound trite, but it is true.

No matter who the artist is that you most admire, no matter what painting you love the most, it was once nothing more than a thought that had to be sketched out…

Sketches are not, in themselves, finished drawings. They are practice for a finished product, or just a musing to get onto paper for later analysis…

There is no such thing as a bad sketch. Some sketches will naturally come to life while others just fizzle out, it all depends on how much thought, time, and energy is put into it…

Sketch from life by looking at something and drawing what you see, or just use your imagination and create stuff!

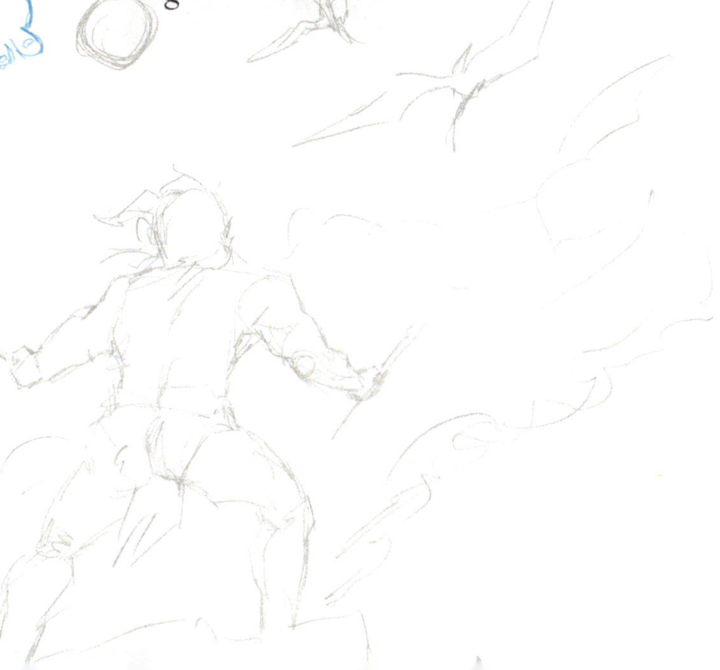

Carry a sketchpad everywhere with you, sketch everything and anything you see or feel!

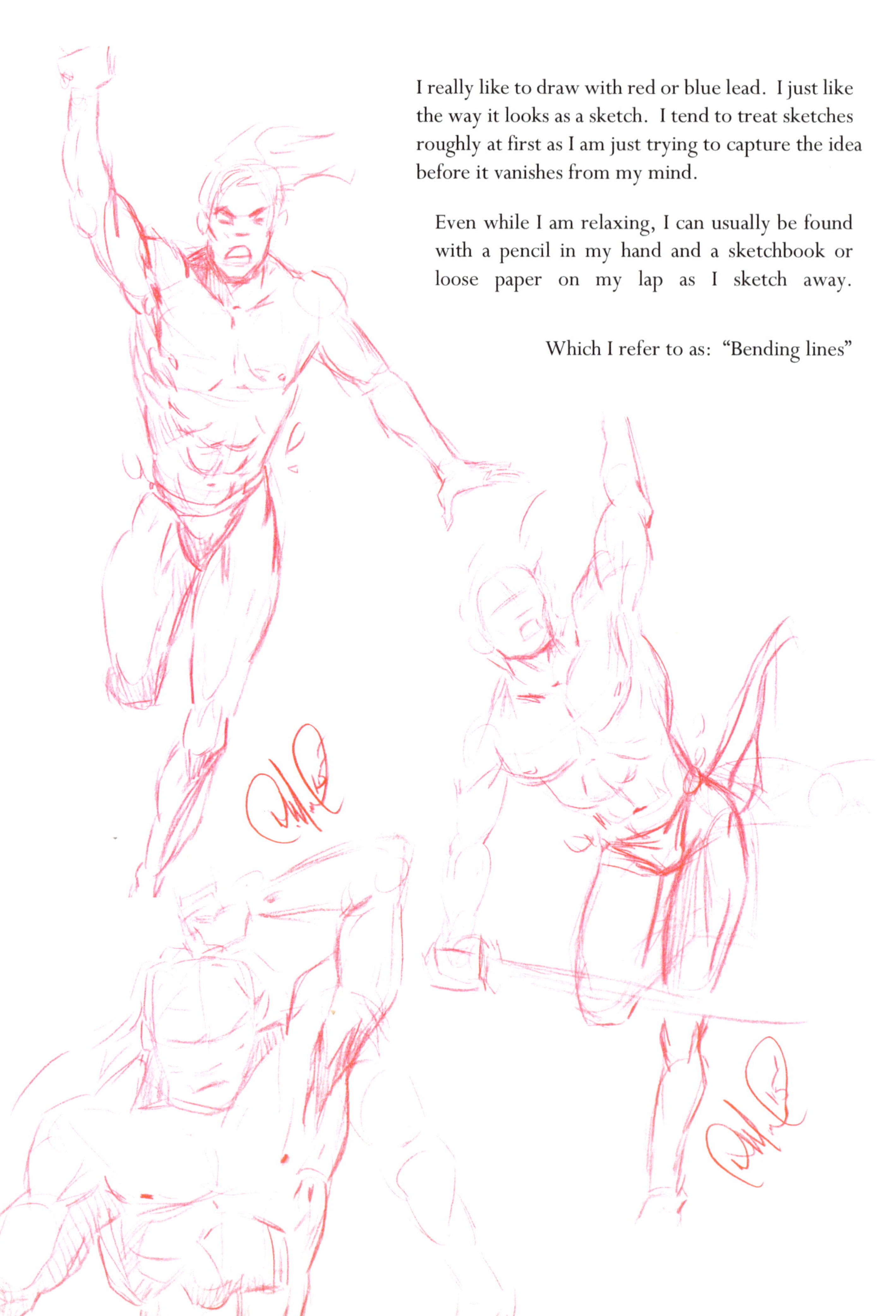

I really like to draw with red or blue lead. I just like the way it looks as a sketch. I tend to treat sketches roughly at first as I am just trying to capture the idea before it vanishes from my mind.

Even while I am relaxing, I can usually be found with a pencil in my hand and a sketchbook or loose paper on my lap as I sketch away.

Which I refer to as: "Bending lines"

I often plot out my paintings with these type of ink and marker sketches. Complete with notes around the margins.

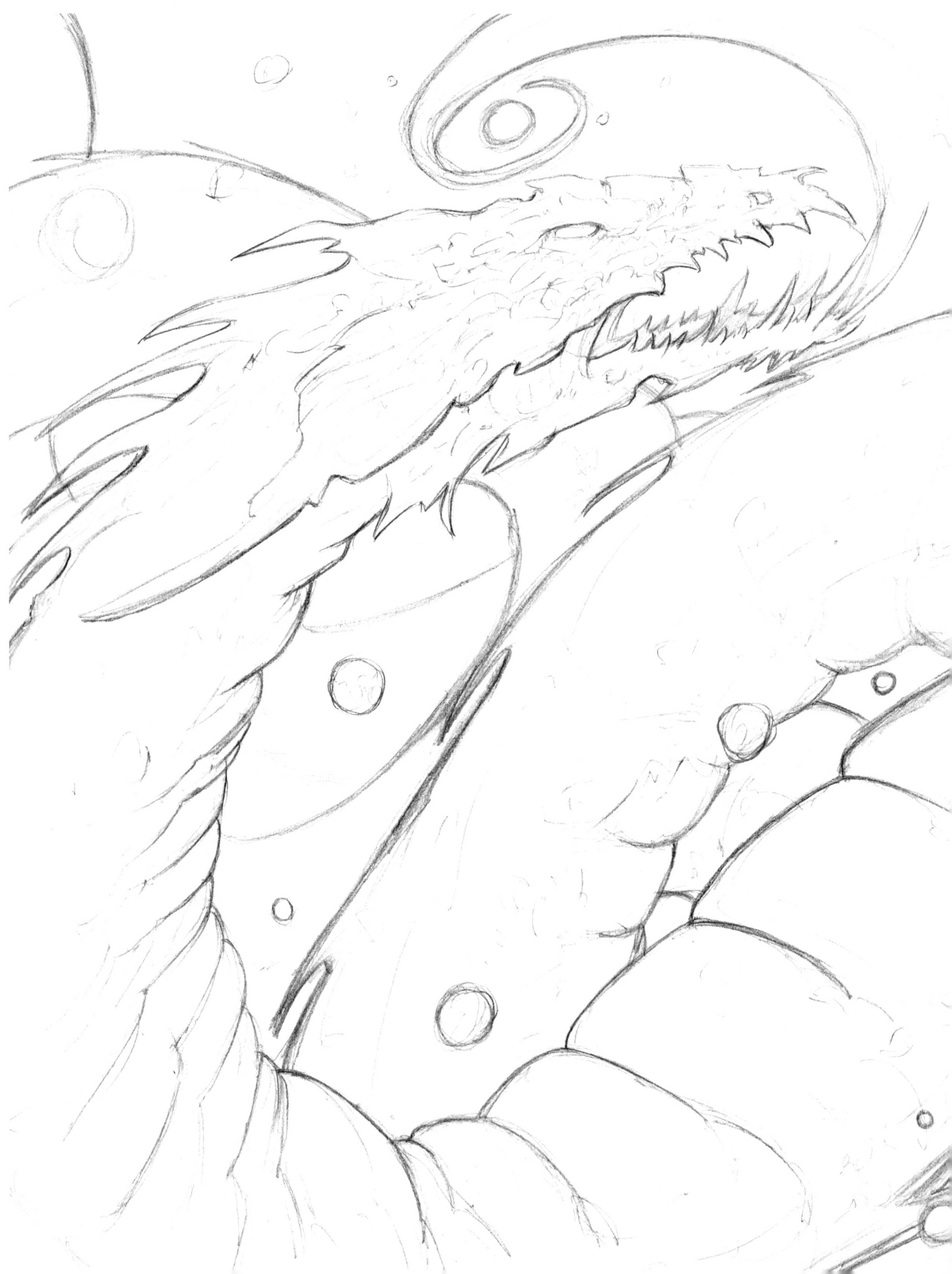

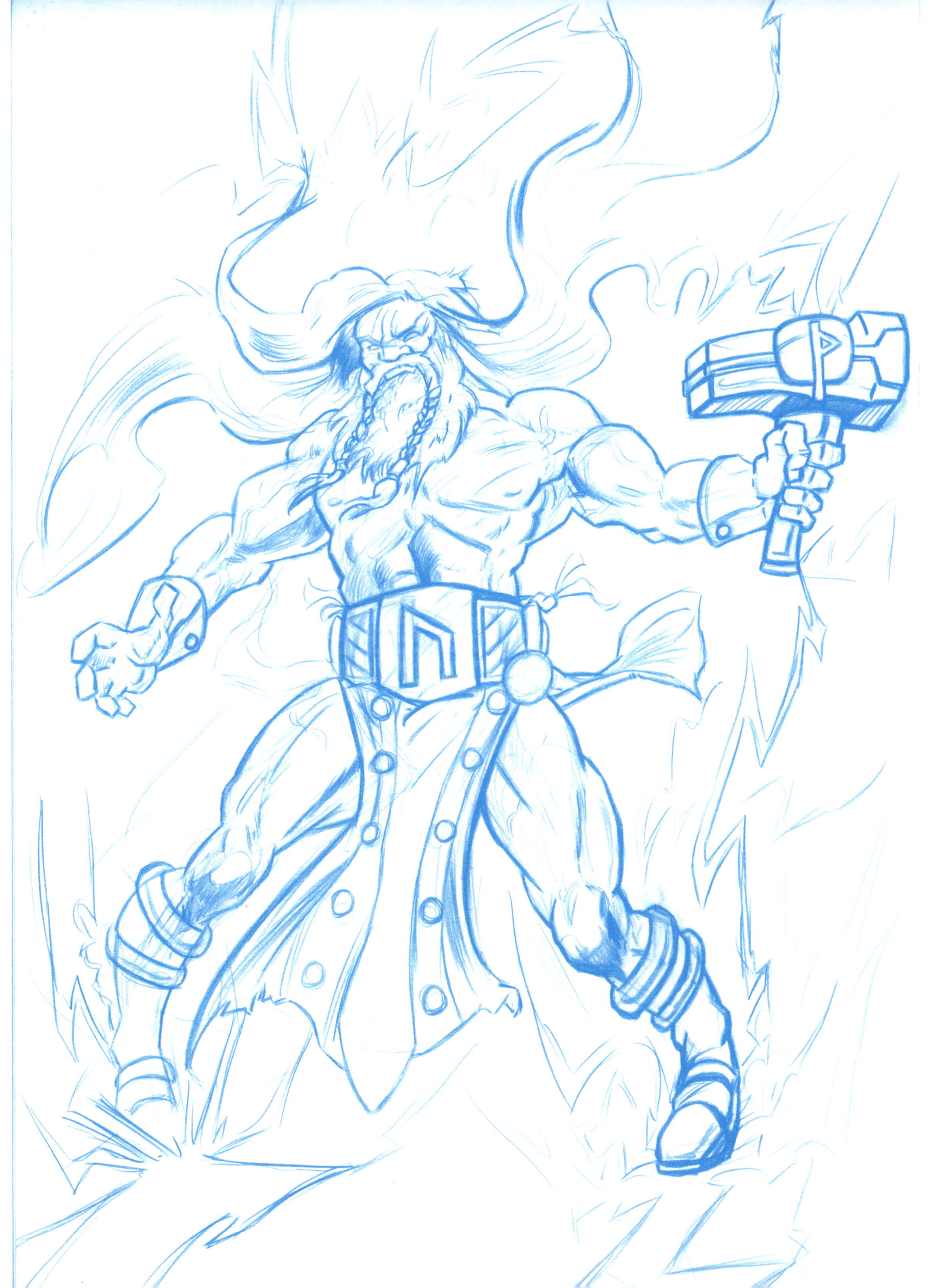

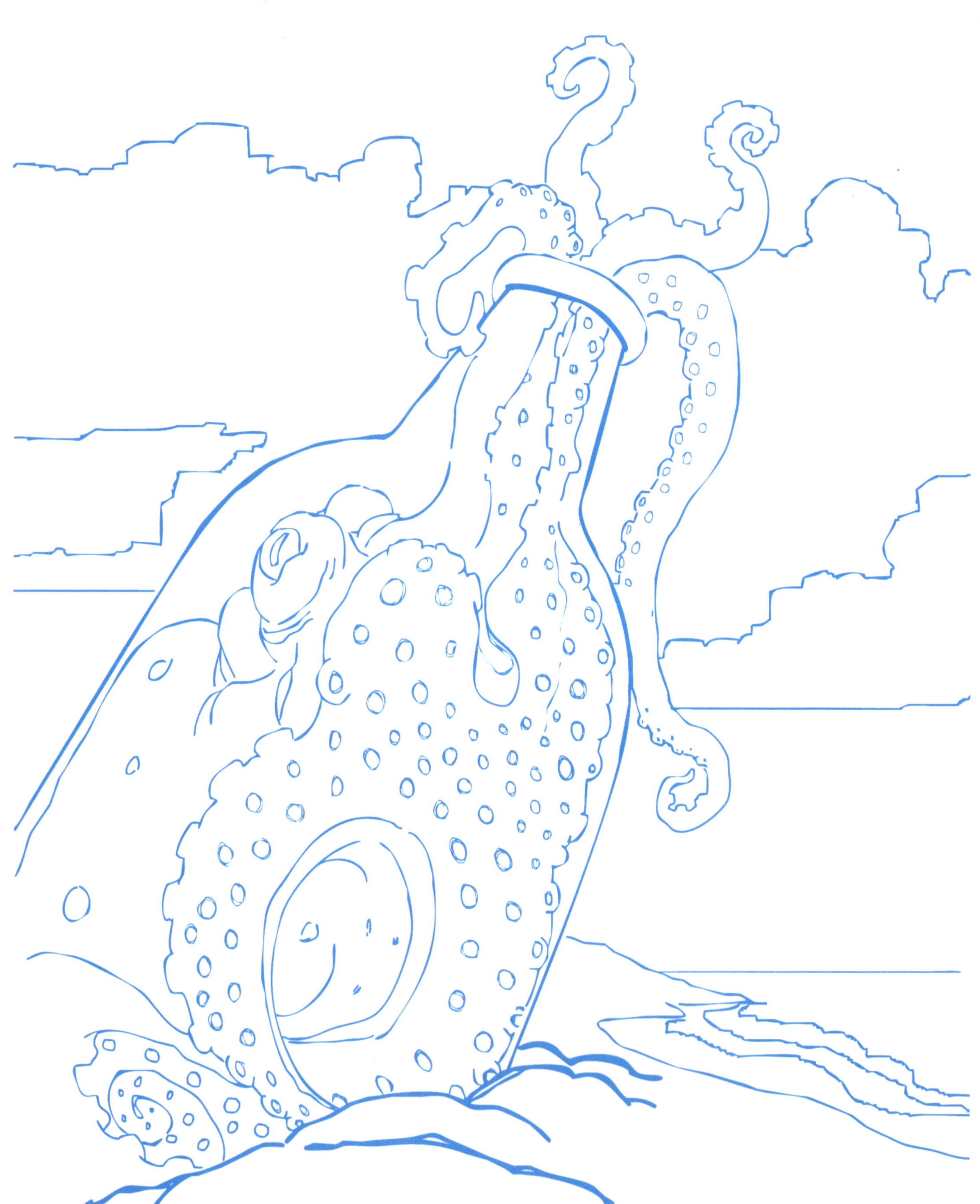

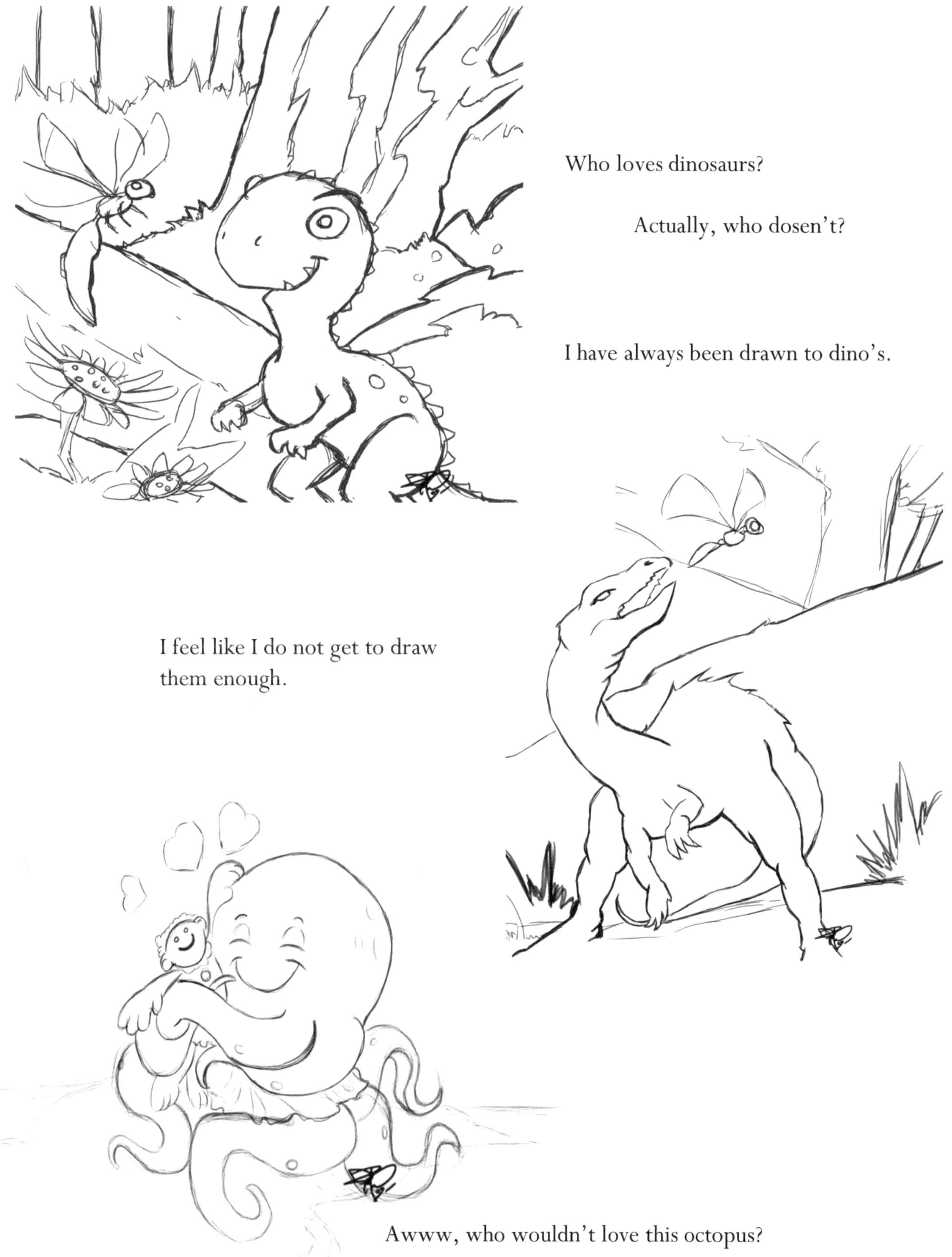

Who loves dinosaurs?

Actually, who dosen't?

I have always been drawn to dino's.

I feel like I do not get to draw them enough.

Awww, who wouldn't love this octopus?

Pigeon drawings 2015

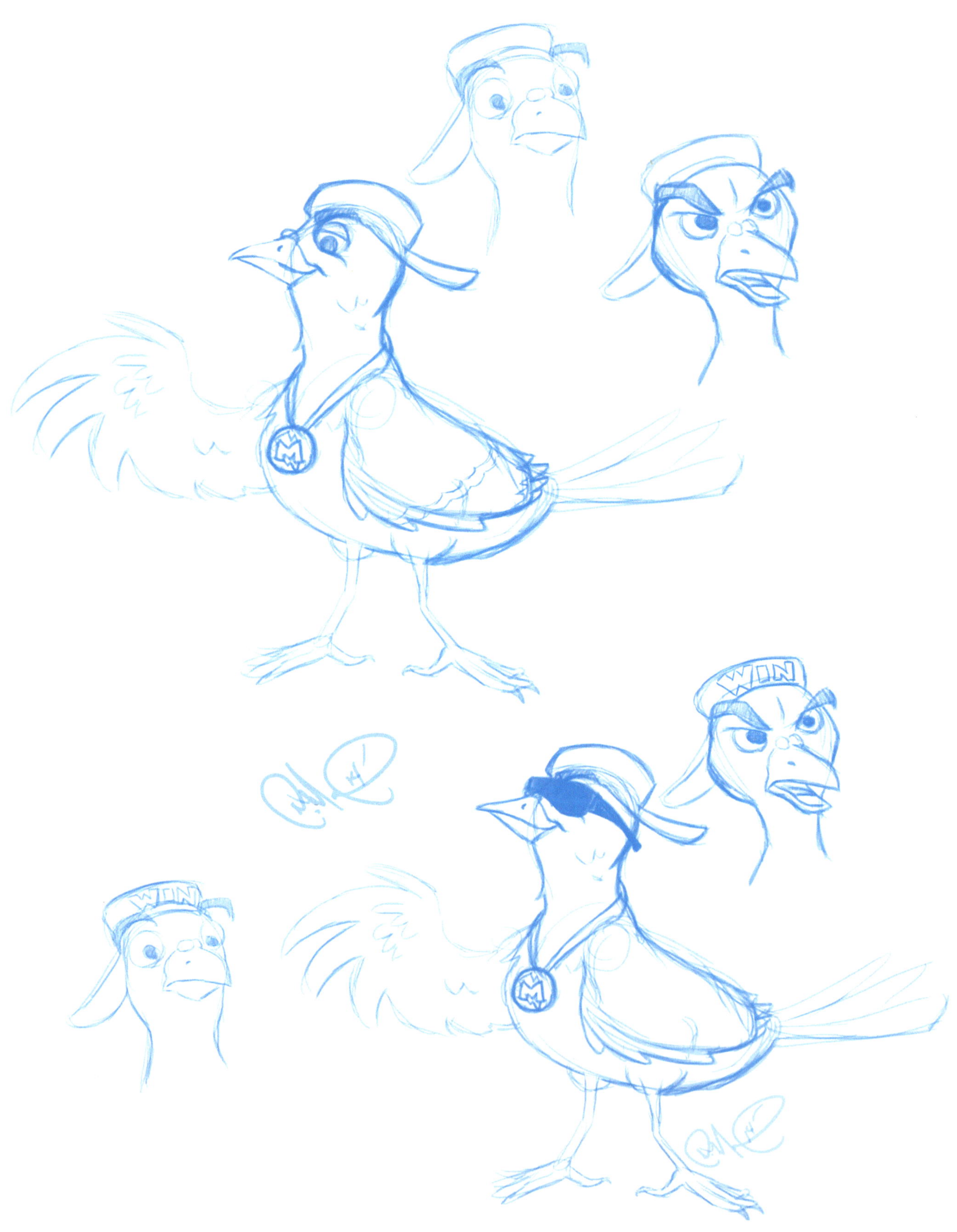

Character design sheet

Artist: Dan Monroe
Character: Mario

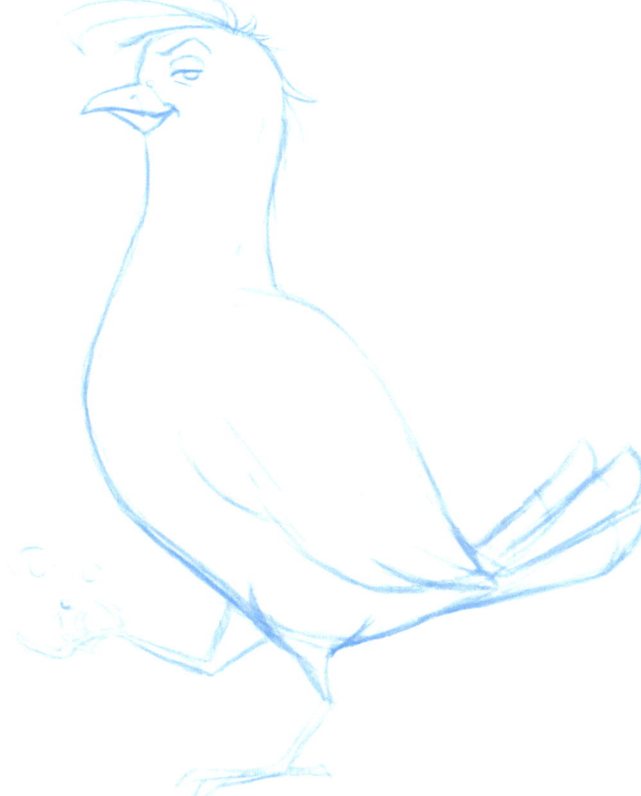

Character design art copyright ©2014 Dan Monroe

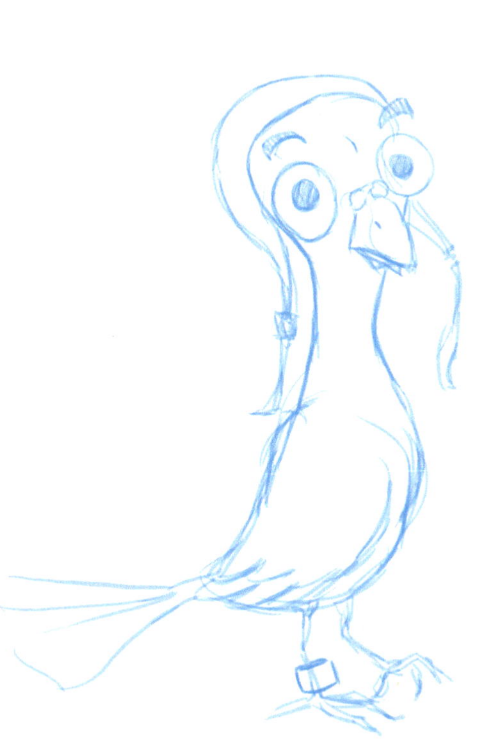

On the previous page you will see the beginnings of the sketches which became this character. The client did not care for the initial sketches and so I played around with the concept until the character was created to the client's satisfaction, unfortunately this project was never fully realized for a variety of reasons.

I really did enjoy doing these drawings, as I had never been asked to draw pigeons before.

Since the project fell flat, I immediately filed the copyright of these characters with the Library of Congress to protect myself, and maintain the integrity of the designs.

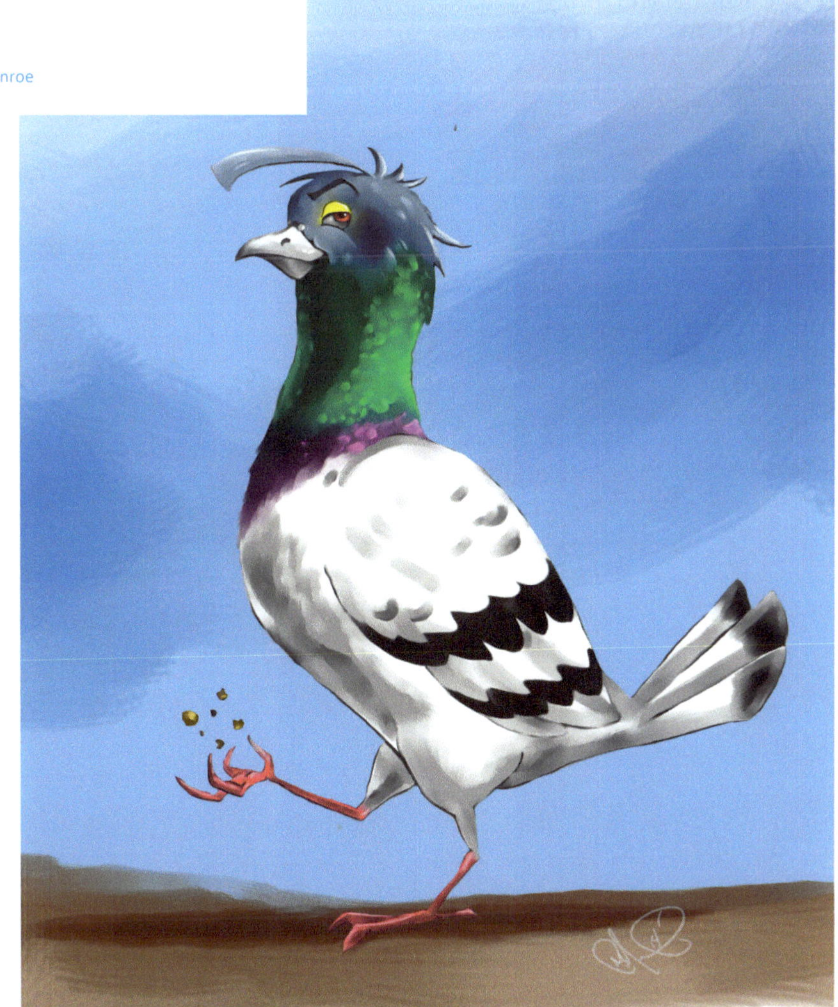

More character sketches for the pigeon project.

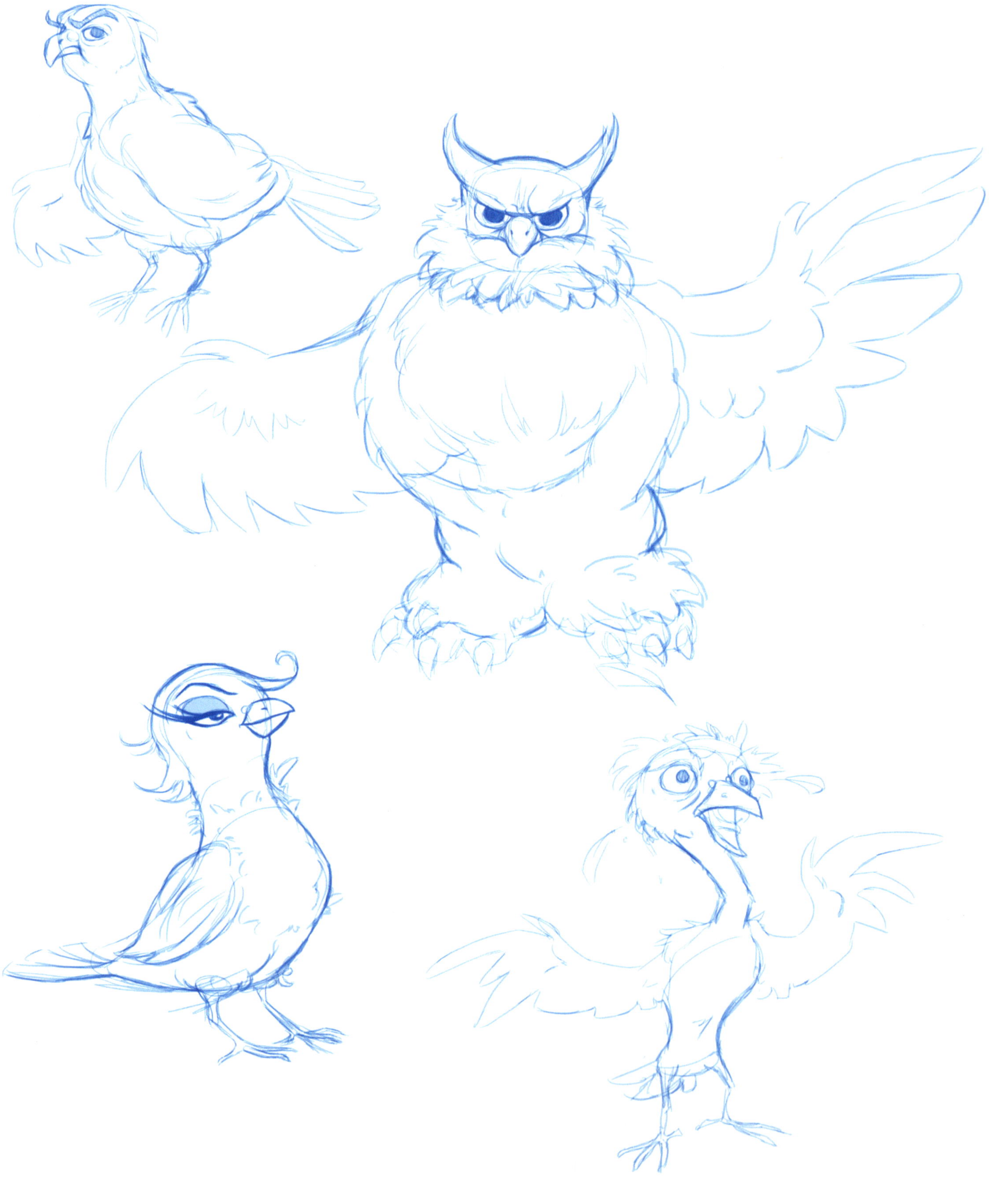

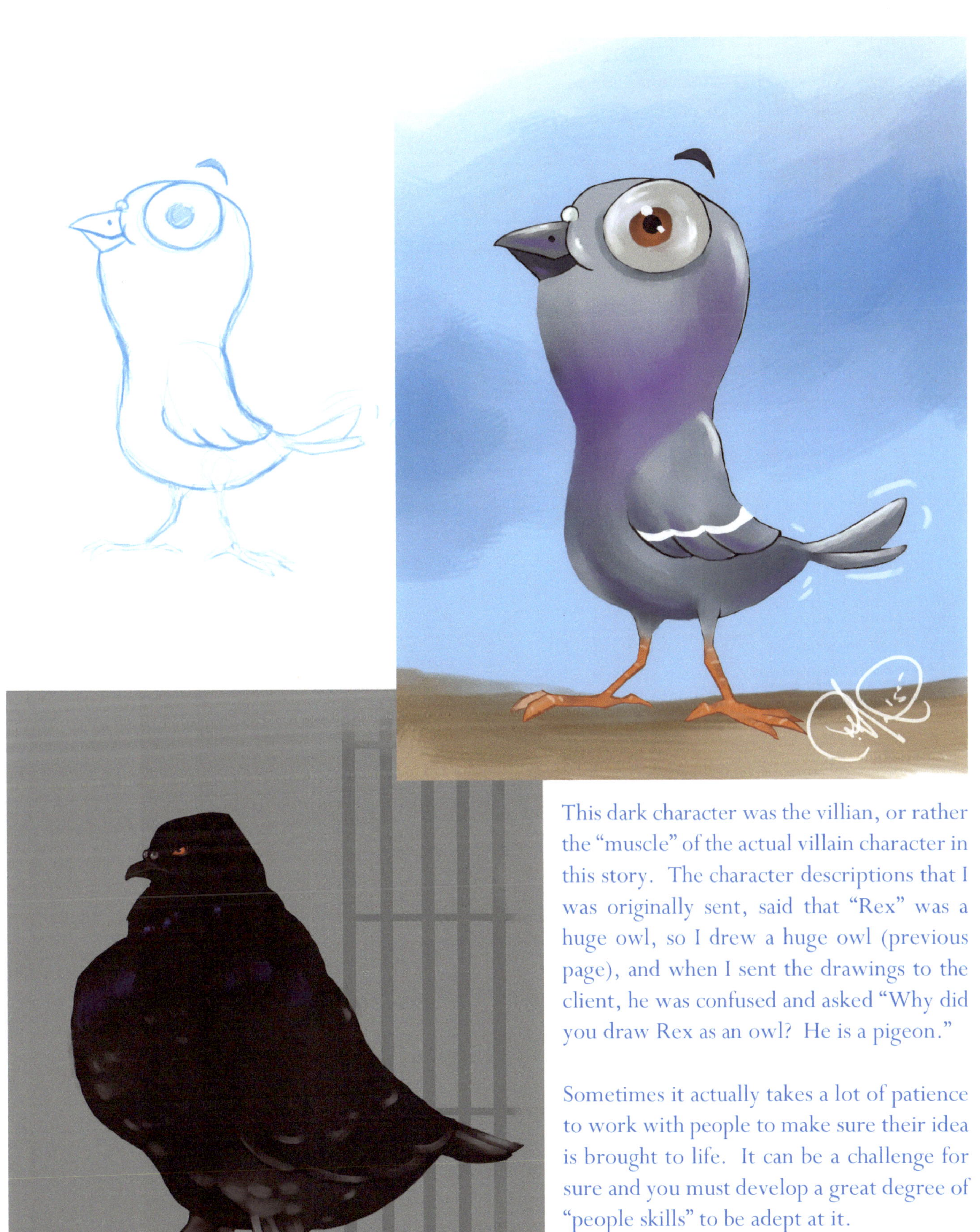

This dark character was the villian, or rather the "muscle" of the actual villain character in this story. The character descriptions that I was originally sent, said that "Rex" was a huge owl, so I drew a huge owl (previous page), and when I sent the drawings to the client, he was confused and asked "Why did you draw Rex as an owl? He is a pigeon."

Sometimes it actually takes a lot of patience to work with people to make sure their idea is brought to life. It can be a challenge for sure and you must develop a great degree of "people skills" to be adept at it.

It is good to ask many questions. Most of the time the client does not know what you need, it is up to you to find out.

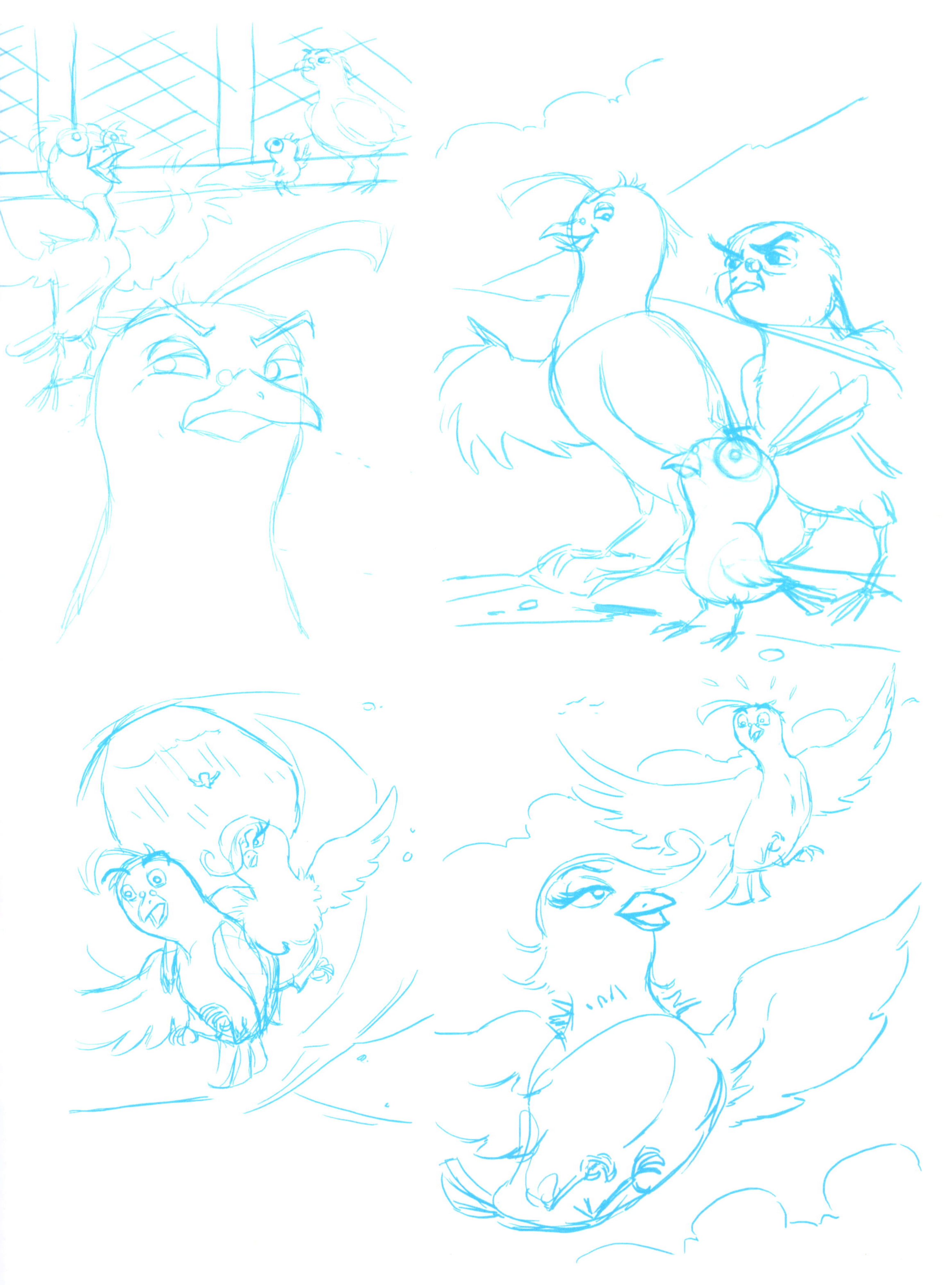

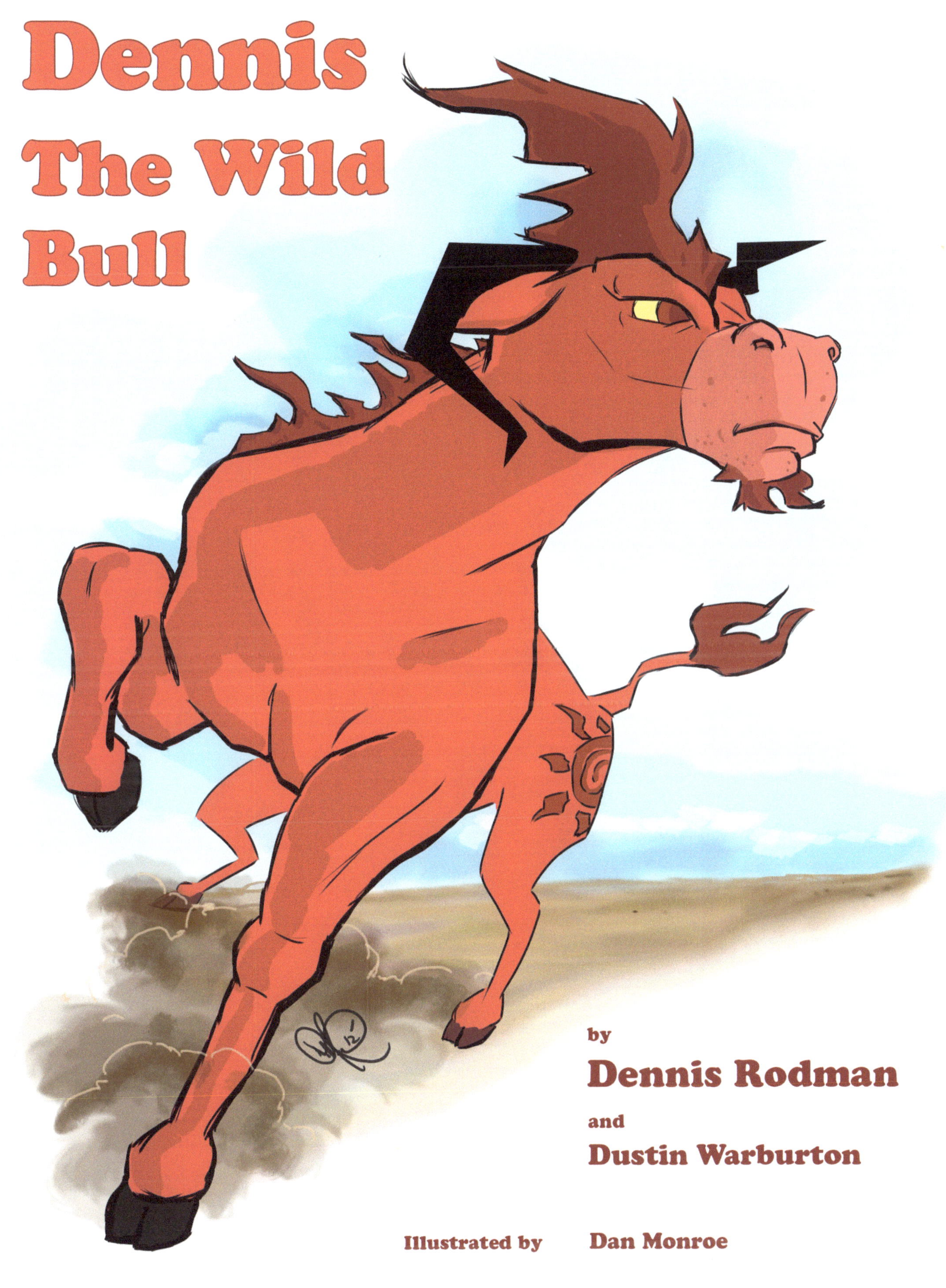

Dennis
The Wild
Bull
by
Dennis Rodman
and
Dustin Warburton
Illustrated by   Dan Monroe

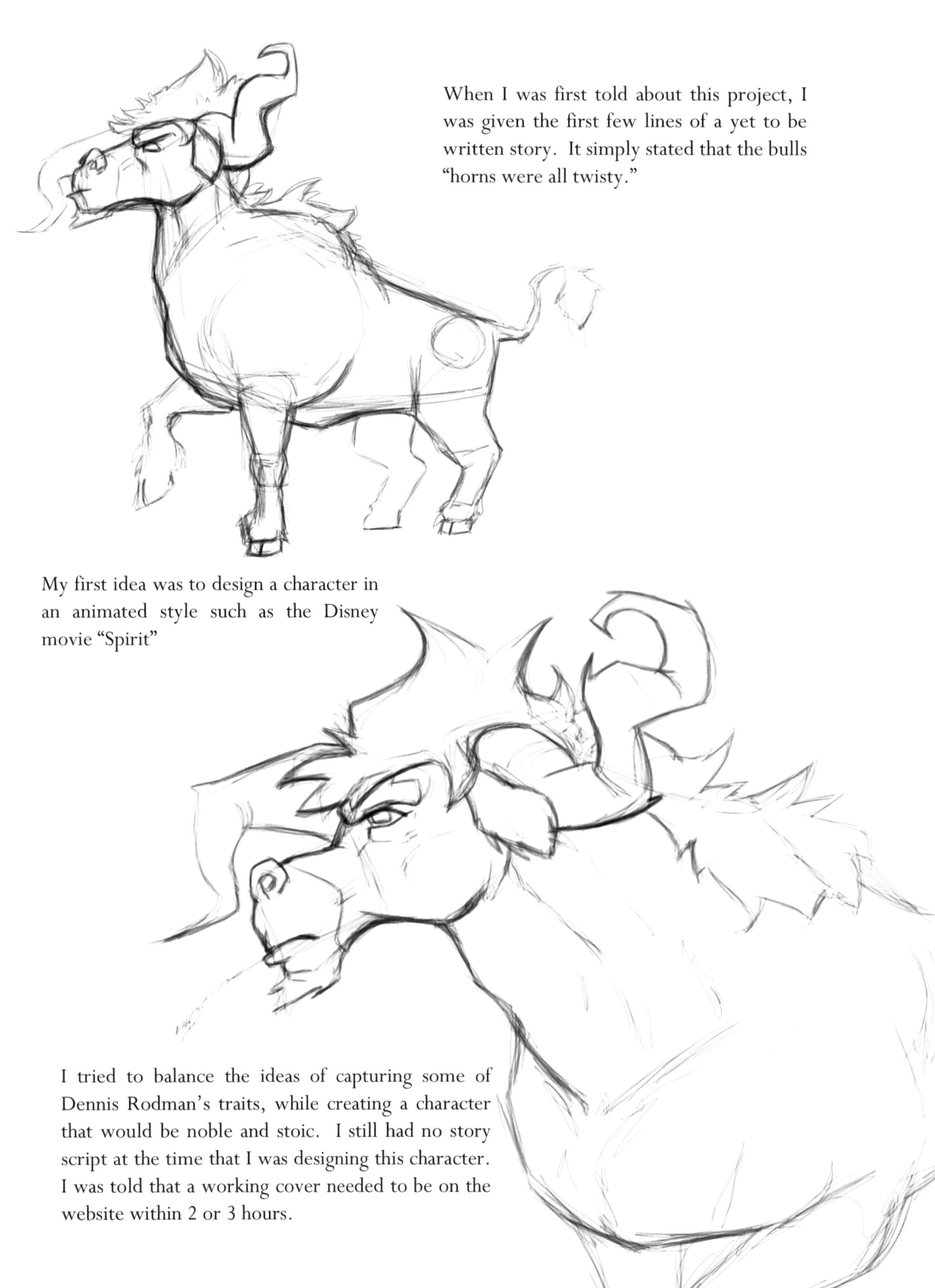

When I was first told about this project, I was given the first few lines of a yet to be written story. It simply stated that the bulls "horns were all twisty."

My first idea was to design a character in an animated style such as the Disney movie "Spirit"

I tried to balance the ideas of capturing some of Dennis Rodman's traits, while creating a character that would be noble and stoic. I still had no story script at the time that I was designing this character. I was told that a working cover needed to be on the website within 2 or 3 hours.

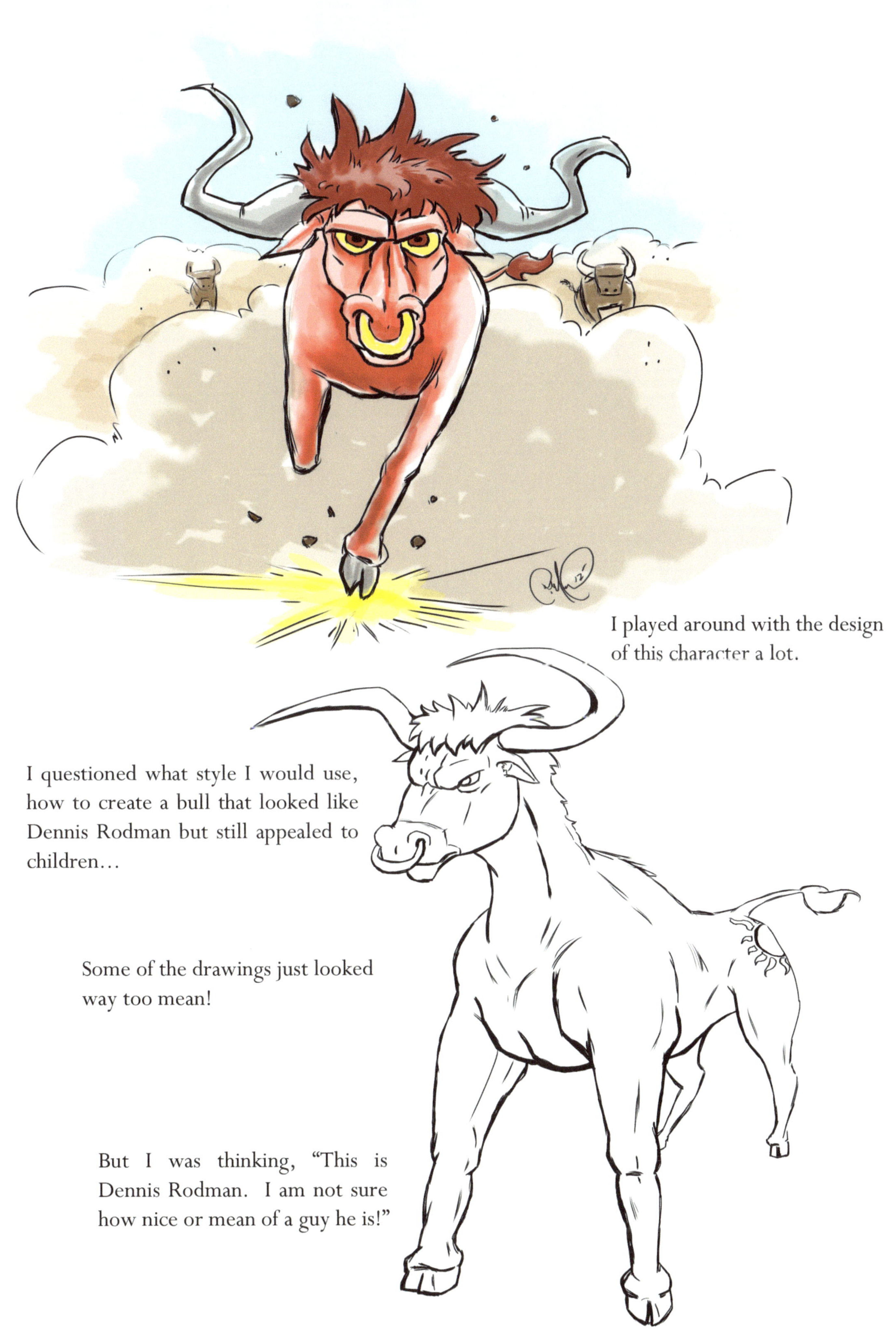

I played around with the design of this character a lot.

I questioned what style I would use, how to create a bull that looked like Dennis Rodman but still appealed to children…

Some of the drawings just looked way too mean!

But I was thinking, "This is Dennis Rodman. I am not sure how nice or mean of a guy he is!"

Bull sketch design sheet #2

by

Dan Monroe

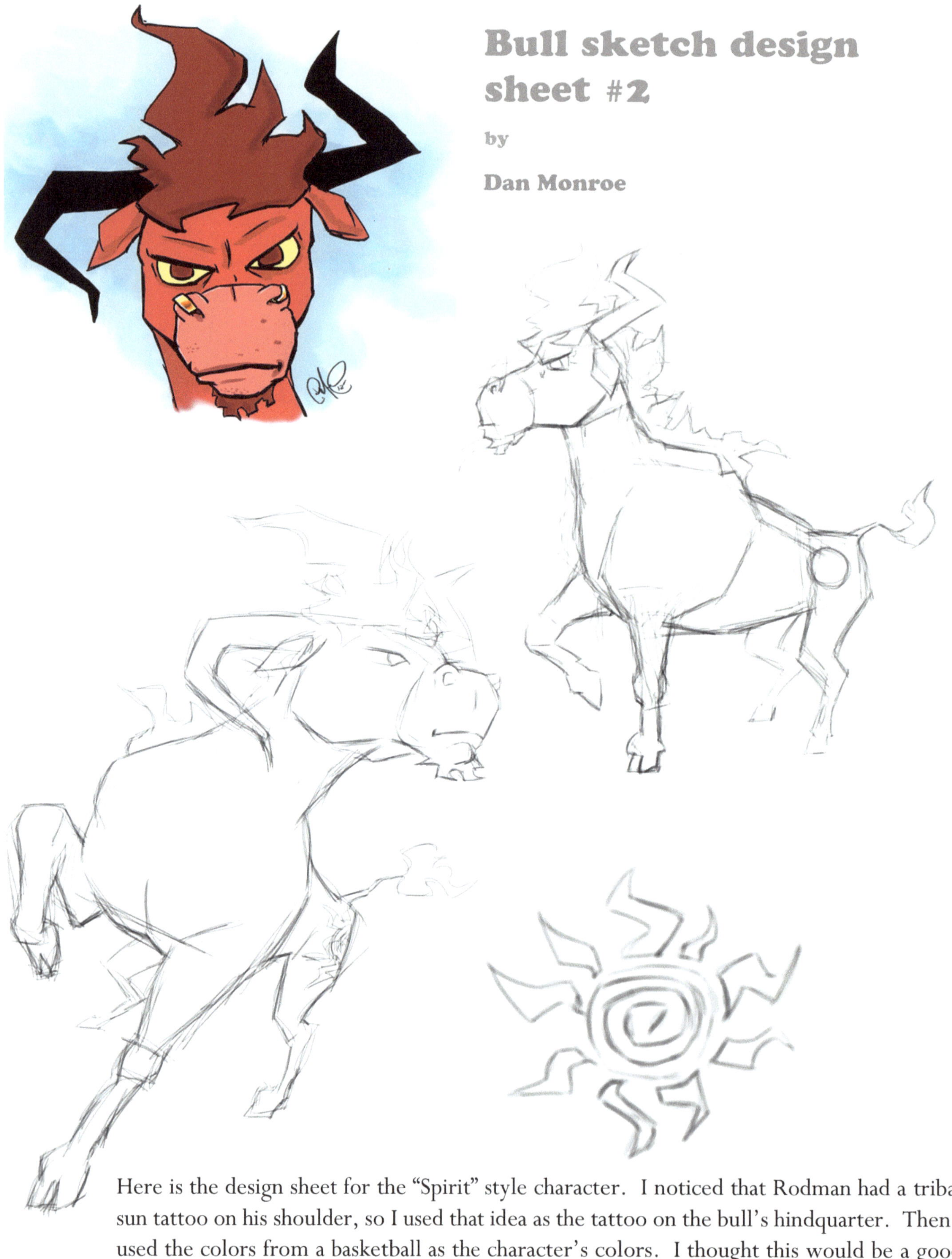

Here is the design sheet for the "Spirit" style character. I noticed that Rodman had a tribal sun tattoo on his shoulder, so I used that idea as the tattoo on the bull's hindquarter. Then I used the colors from a basketball as the character's colors. I thought this would be a good way to acknowledge his career. I am not sure anyone ever understood it though, or cared.

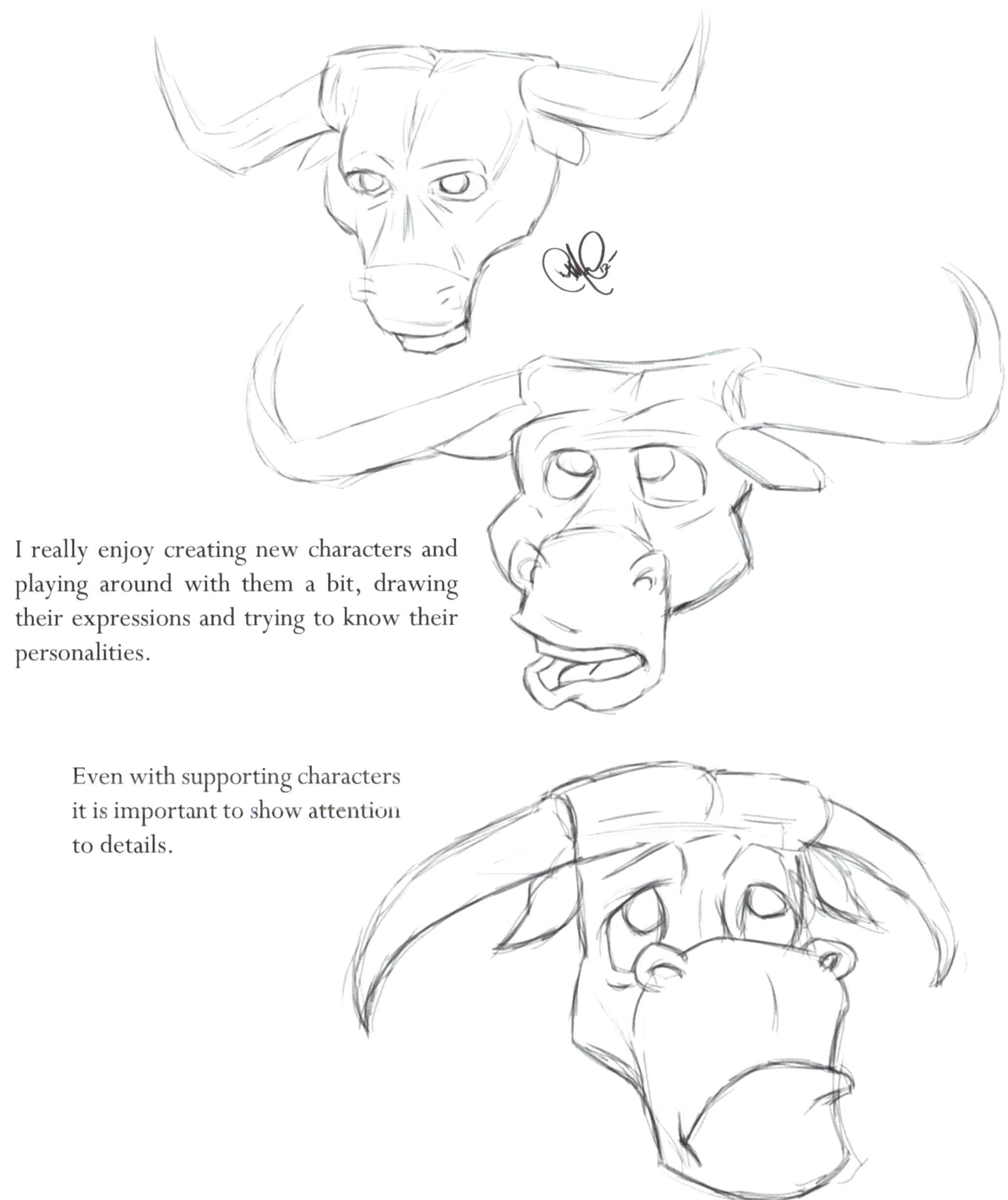

I really enjoy creating new characters and playing around with them a bit, drawing their expressions and trying to know their personalities.

Even with supporting characters it is important to show attention to details.

I was never given any direction on the creation of any of these characters until the point when an entirely new script was sent to me. In that script I was given some small description about Pedro being a "Mexican with a mustache and pudgy", and Benny being a "Smallish white bull." I was actually mortified and disturbed by the description that I was sent as I felt it was not in the best light. I let my feelings be known to the guy who sent it- A Johny-come-lately type who felt like he rushed in to save the project because the writer had blown it. However, I did as the client asked because I trusted in good faith that I would be paid for my work.

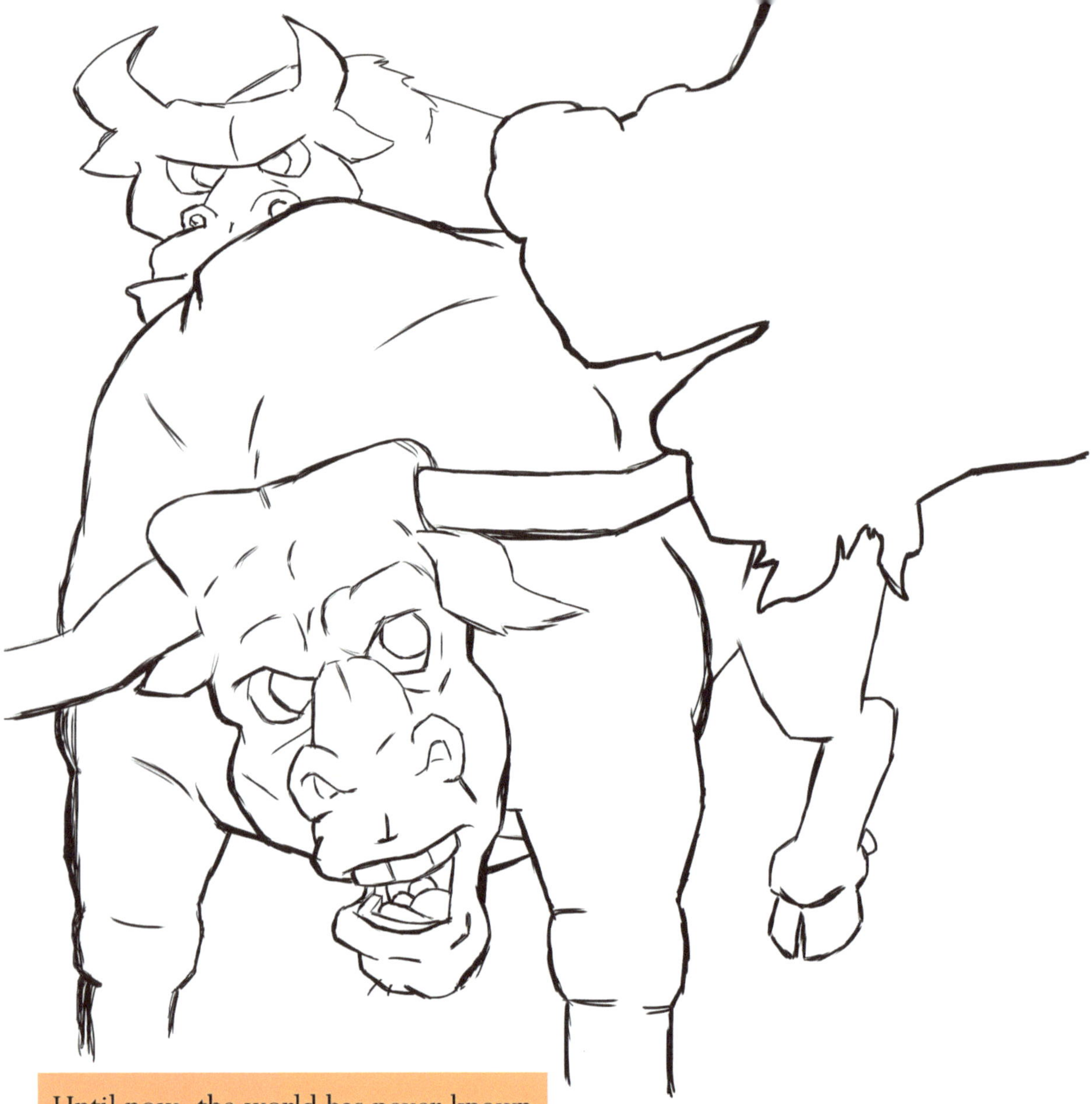

Until now, the world has never known the saga of this project- how there are two versions of the book. The book which was published, and the first draft which was not. In my opinion the original script was poorly written and conceived, however I was led to believe the script was authorized by the Rodman Management team. When the writer sent me the script I questioned it. He assured me that not only was it approved, but the Rodman people "LOVED IT!"

I created all of the illustrations as the writer went on vacation. I later found out the script had been rejected, and never authorized at all.

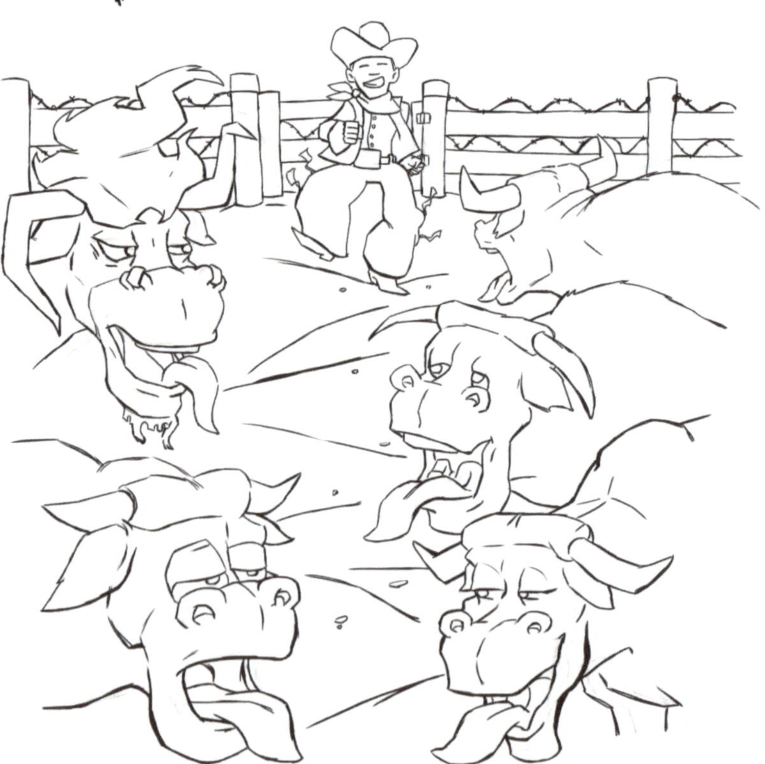

The Rodman team never had a problem with my art- they liked what I was doing, it was just a problem of the story being poorly imagined, in my opinion. The management team told the writer: "We are sure the artist would have no problem working with another writer."

The writer then tried to explain how the illustrator would actually explain a lot of the nuances of the story through his illustrations- which was a way for him to deflect the attention and criticisms for his writing deficiencies. After a time the writer (Or someone, as I am still not exactly sure who wrote the published story) got a script approved, I had to redesign the characters, and went in an entirely new direction while I was at it.

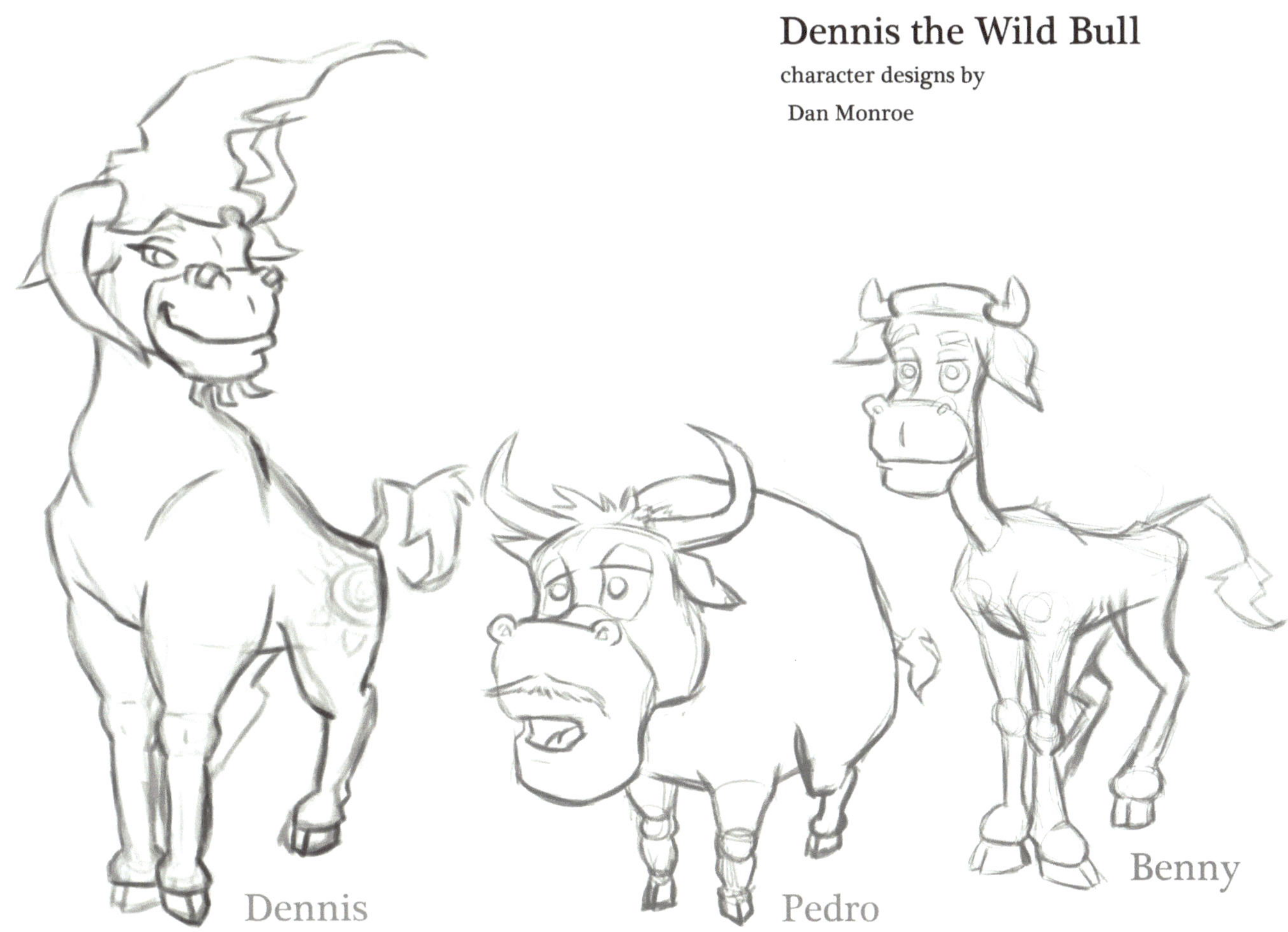

Dennis the Wild Bull

character designs by

Dan Monroe

So, as the world became familiar with the working book cover, and as it was being shown on CNN, and in media sources world-wide, there was an entire drama that unfolded in the creation of it. Perhaps someone will ask me about it someday and I will tell the whole story. To this day I have never been paid a dime for the artwork and creation of this book- which just proves that no matter what, you should always be paid upfront for the work that you do.

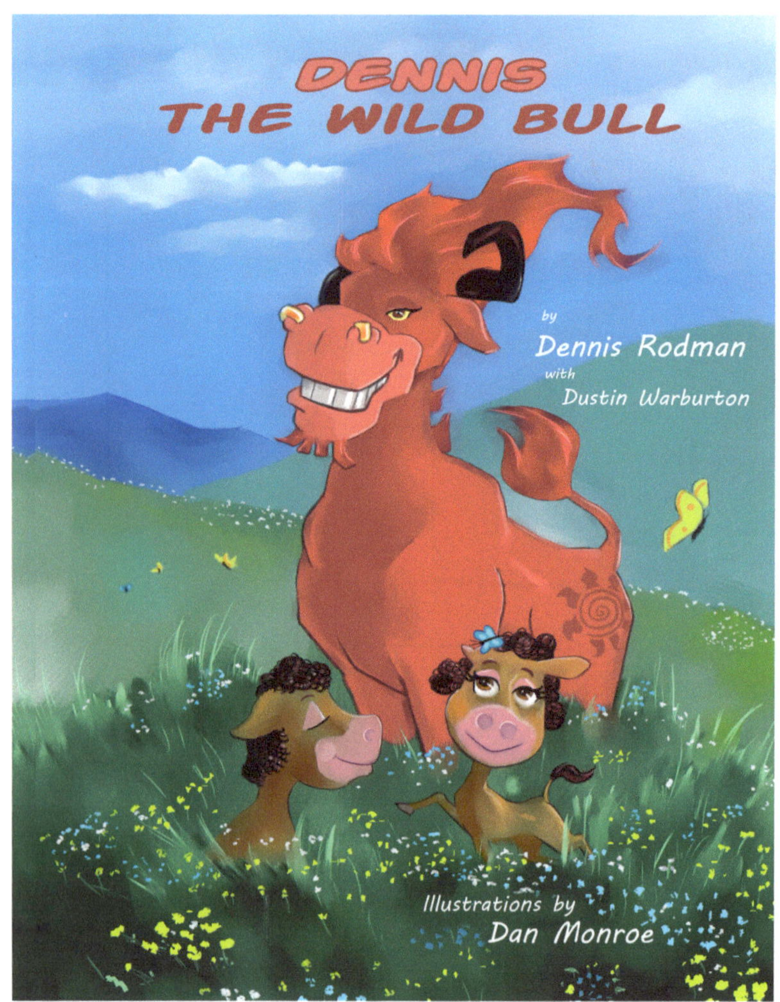

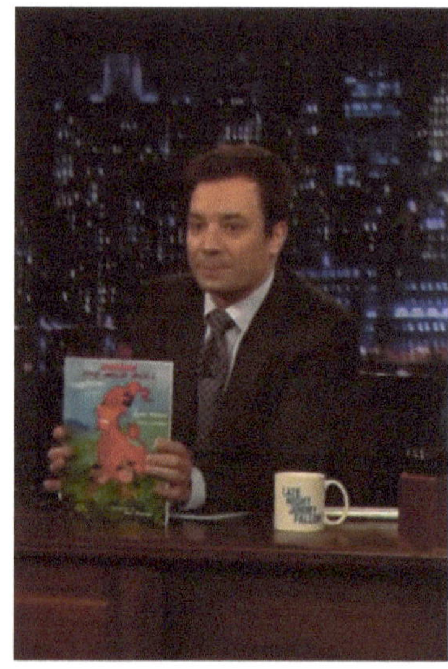

Dennis the Wild Bull was the most anticipated children's book of 2012, and was featured on The Tonight Show with Jay Leno, The Late Show with Jimmy Fallon, on the Oprah Network, and numerous media sources around the globe including TIME. To this day I have never been paid a cent for the work I did on it.

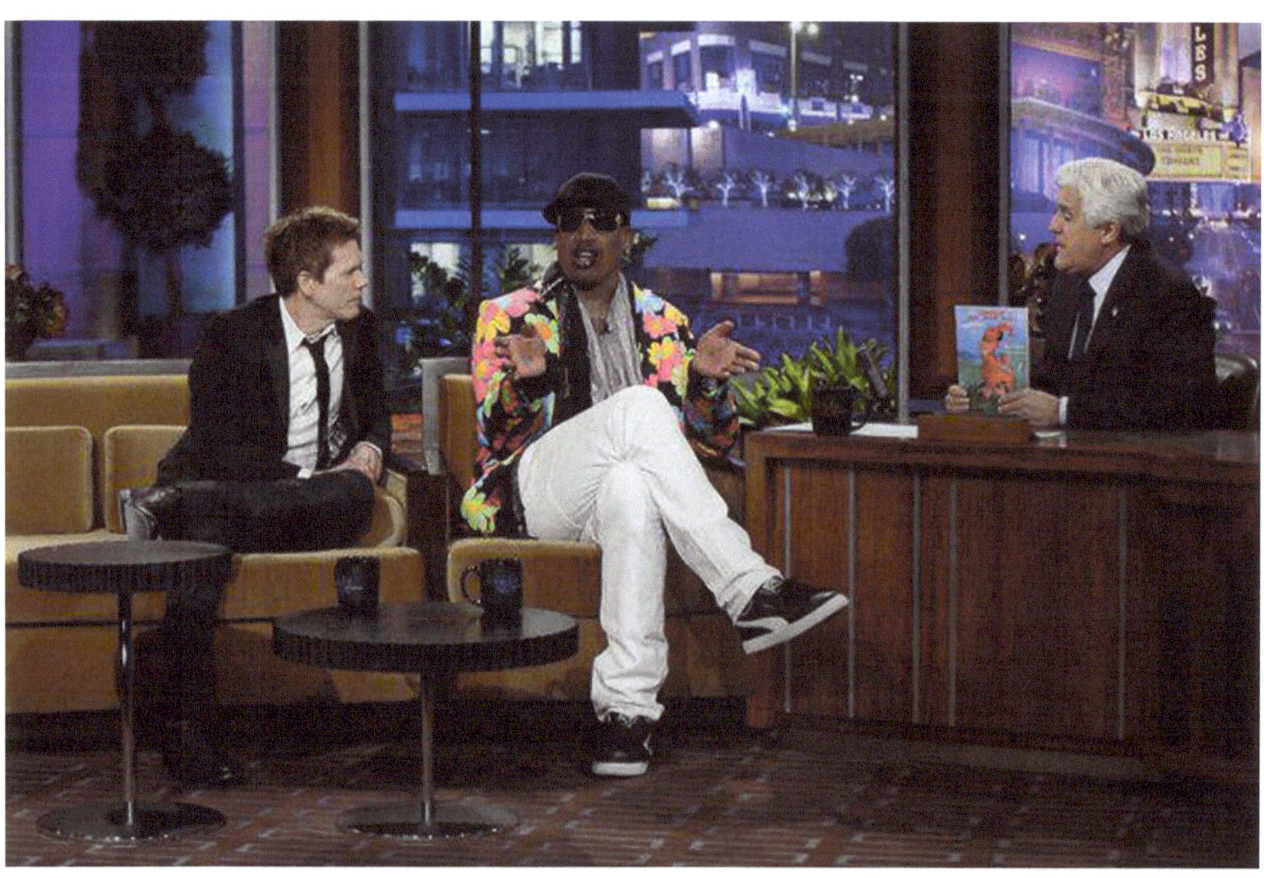

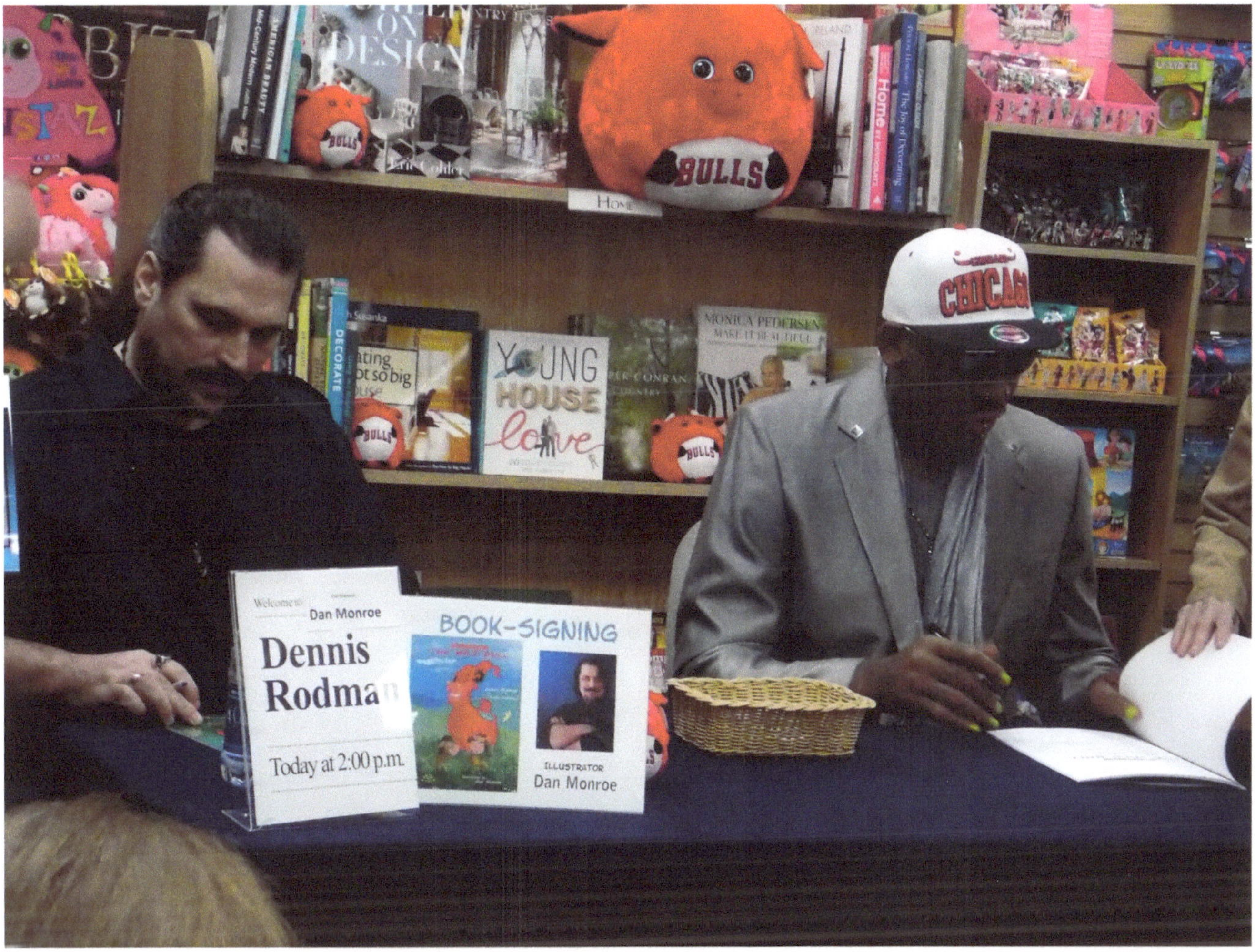

On February 02, 2013 the book made its debut at Anderson's Bookshop in Naperville, IL. I drove for four hours through a horrible blizzard from my home in Michigan in order to attend. I was also carrying books that were shipped to my house as extra's for the bookstore. When I arrived, the bookstore manager asked who I was and when I introduced myself she said, "Well, Rodman should have had someone else write the story, but at least your art is really really good!"

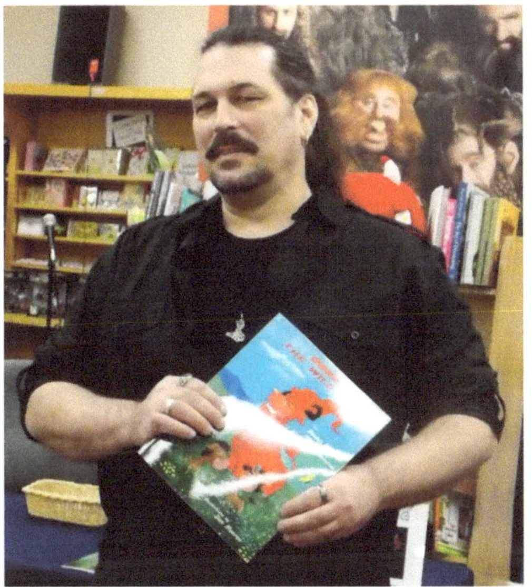

As I sat next to Dennis Rodman to sign books, he looked over at me and said, "Humph! You just had to be here too, huh?" And then ignored me the rest of the time, I just smiled and signed books. I heard some people ask, "Who is that?" and when they were told I was the artist, I would hear them say,,
"Oh, who cares about him? I just want Rodmans autograph!"
There are three copies of the book which have my signature, Rodman's, and Warburton's. I have two of them, the other I gave to a reporter for Sports Illustrated.

Here are some sketches for the book "What To Do When You Lose Your Lalaballoo" by former Baywatch actress Erika Eleniak.

Erika was such a pleasure to work with!

She gave me many idea's about her book and what she wanted to convey.

I would certainly love to work on a project with her again. Perhaps sometime in the future it will happen.

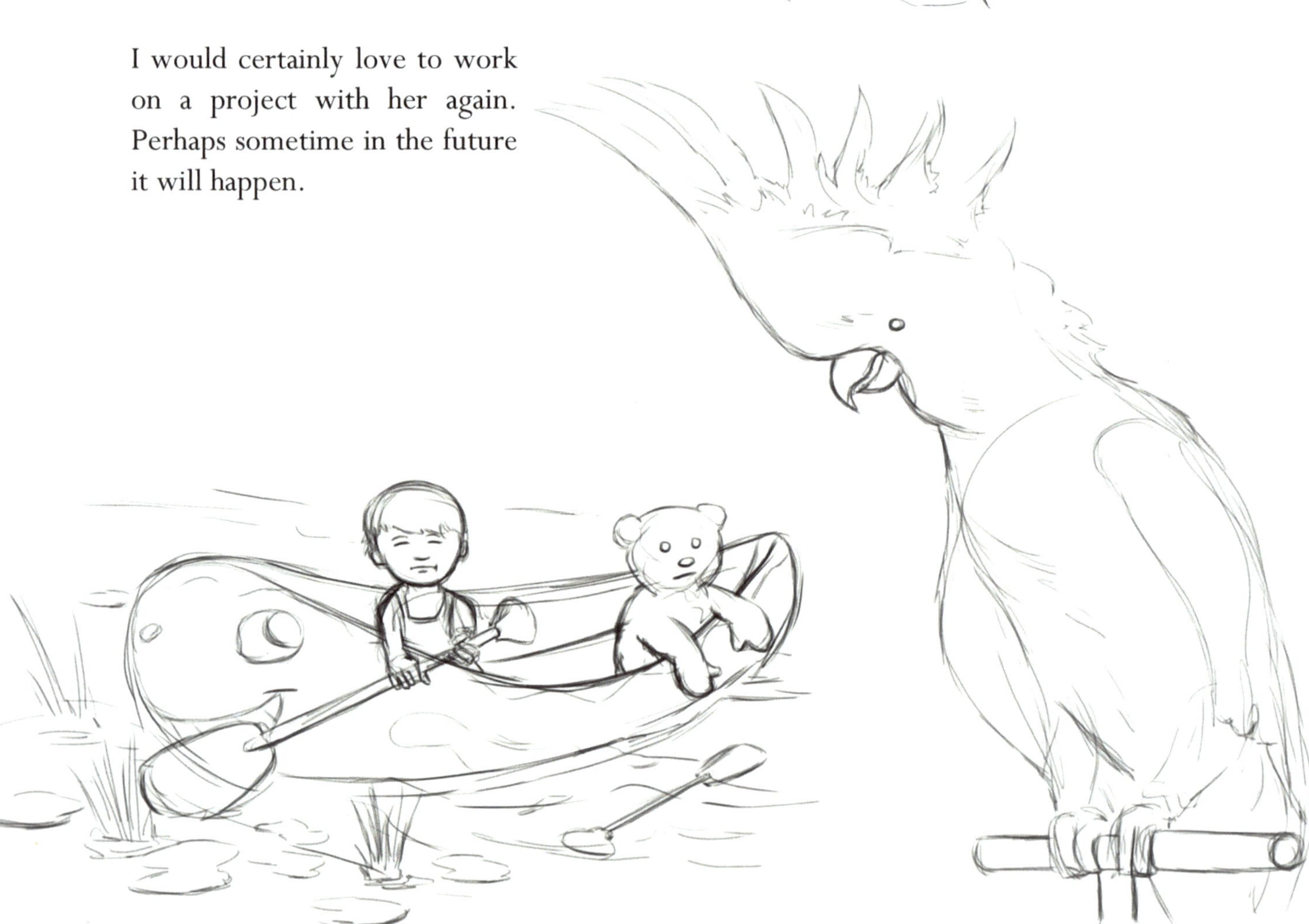

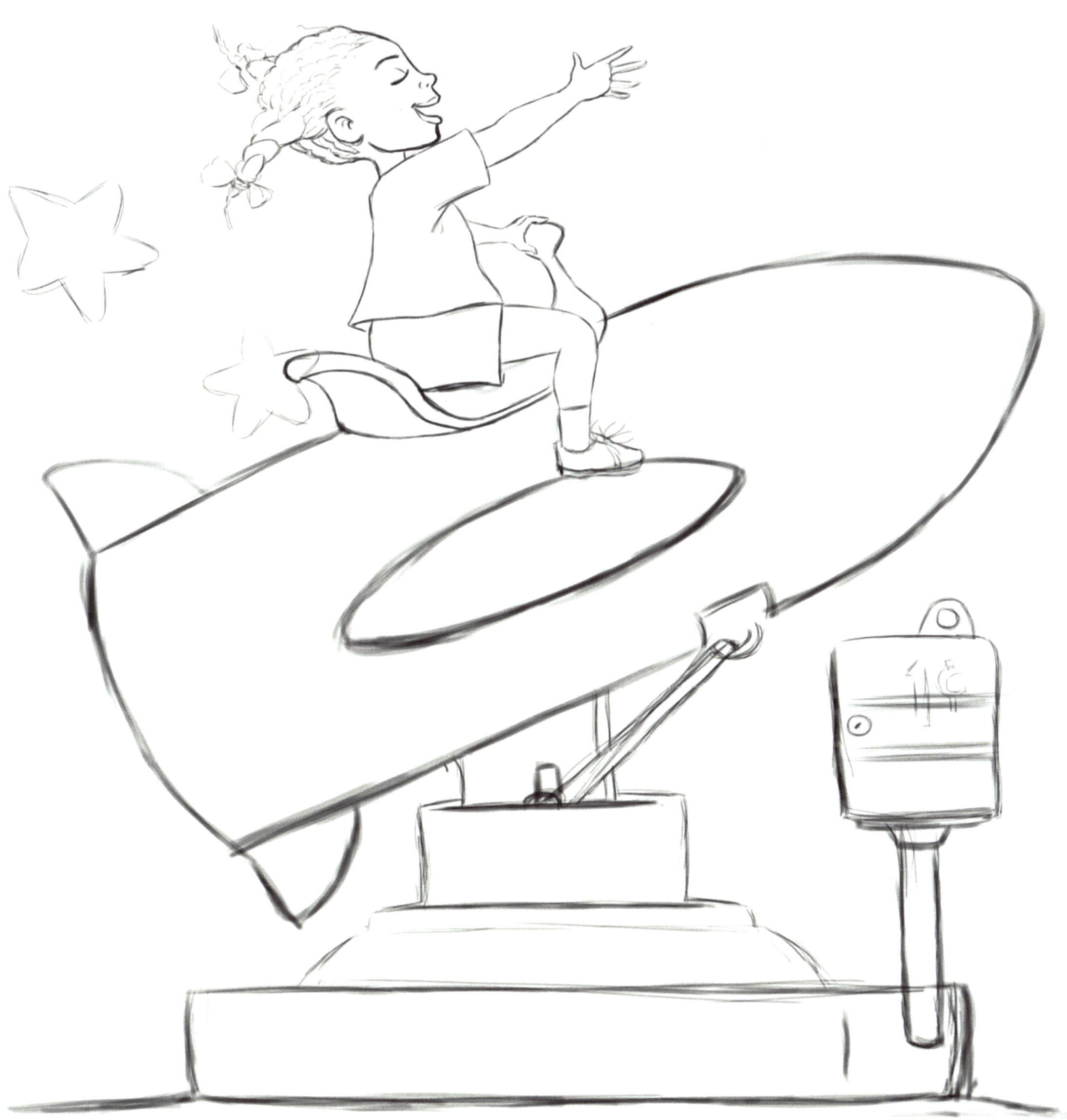

When I read the passage that goes with this drawing, I immediately envisioned this in my mind. A young girl riding a penny-rocket and reaching to the future!

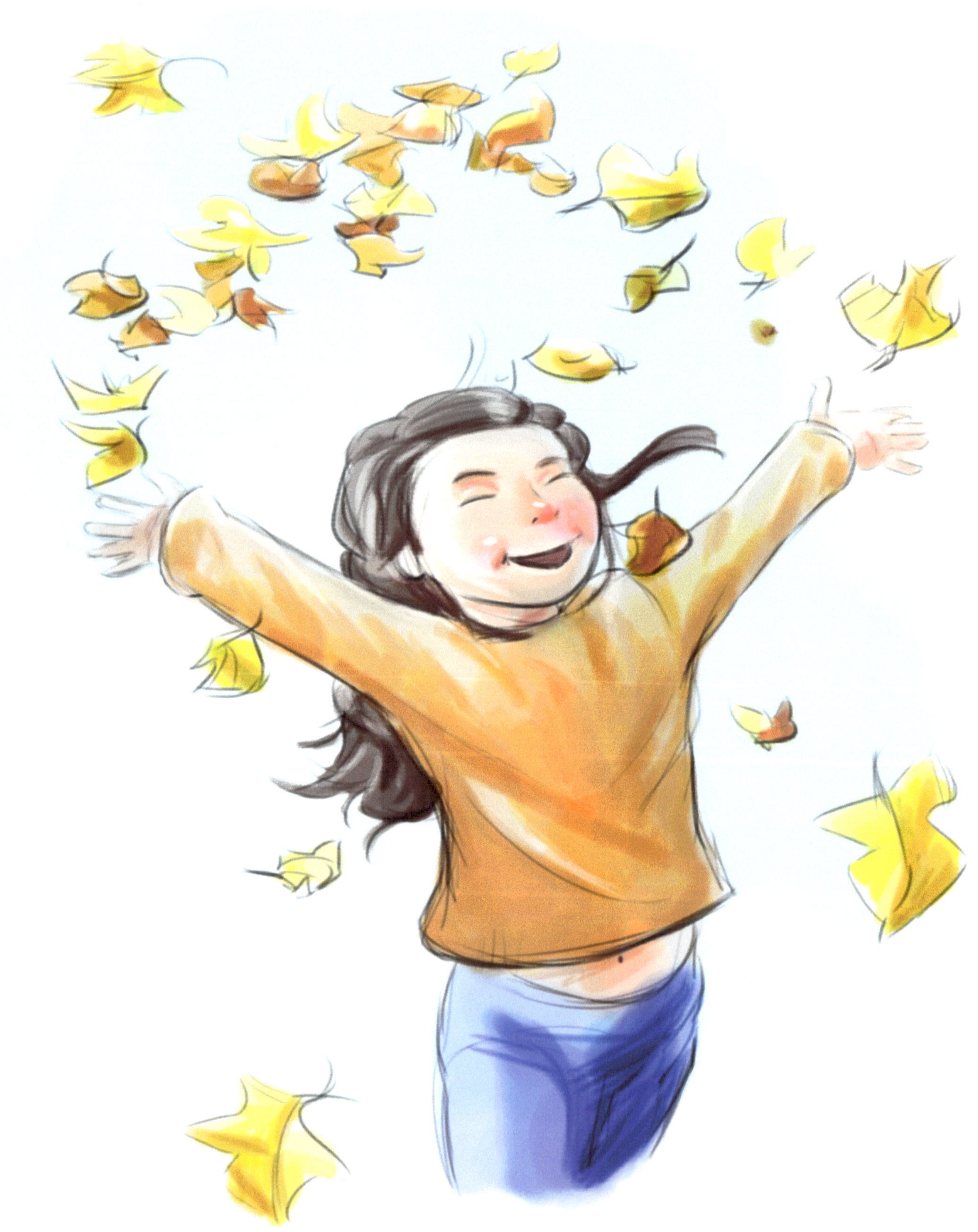

From as early as I can remember, I have always loved to draw monsters. Not always big scary ones, but also the little monsters that children would like. Once again, I believe in as much variety as possible, and you may notice that some of the monsters here even have playful sides to them!

Here you can also see the difference color makes when you add it in.

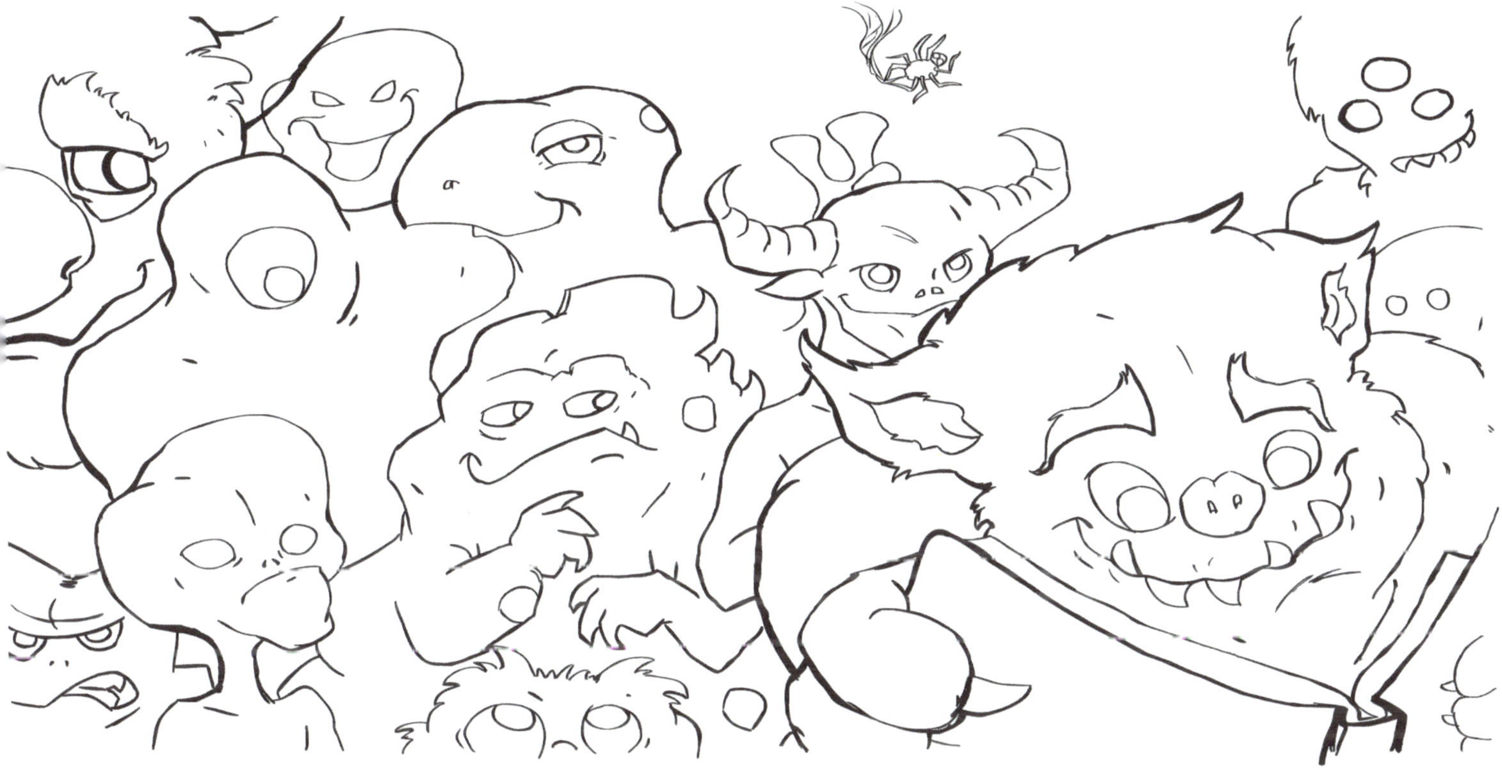

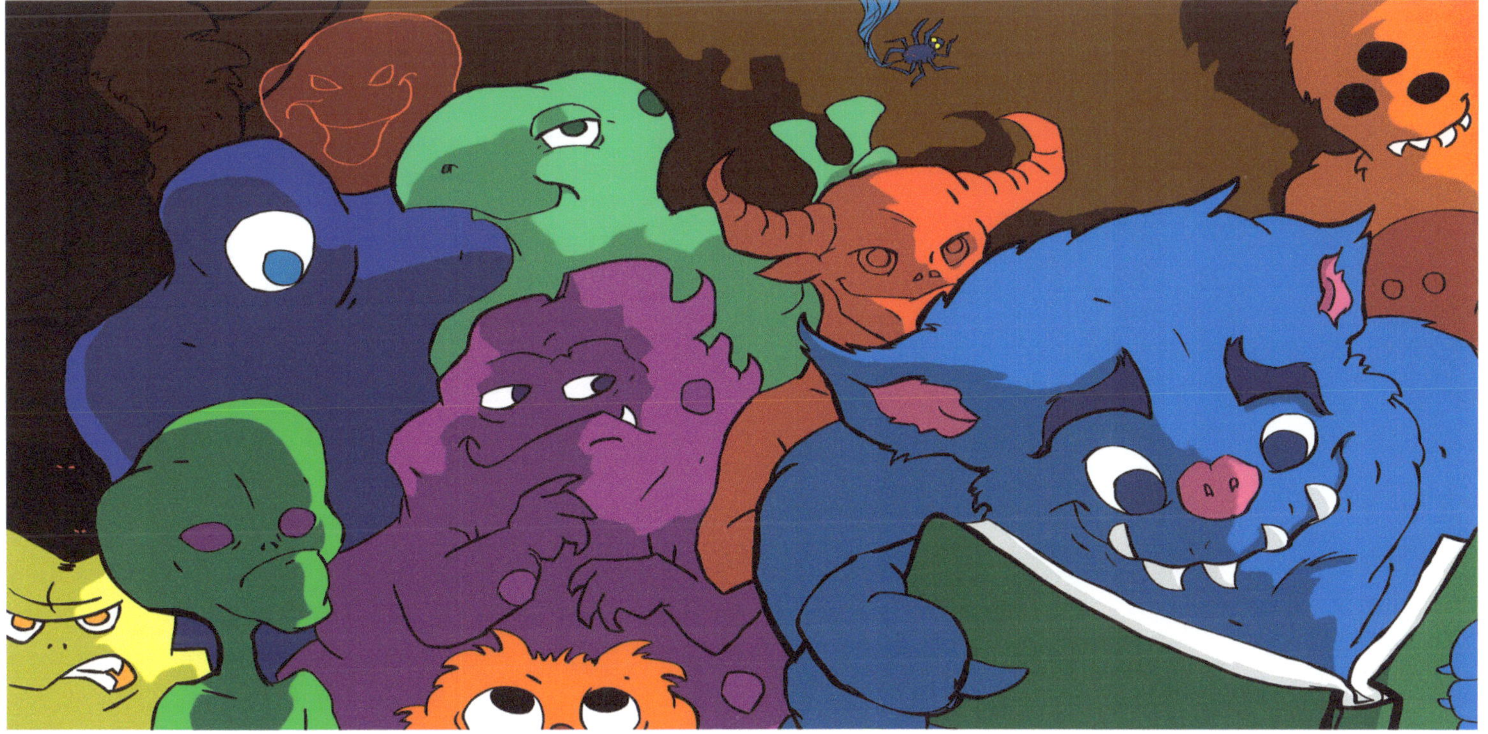

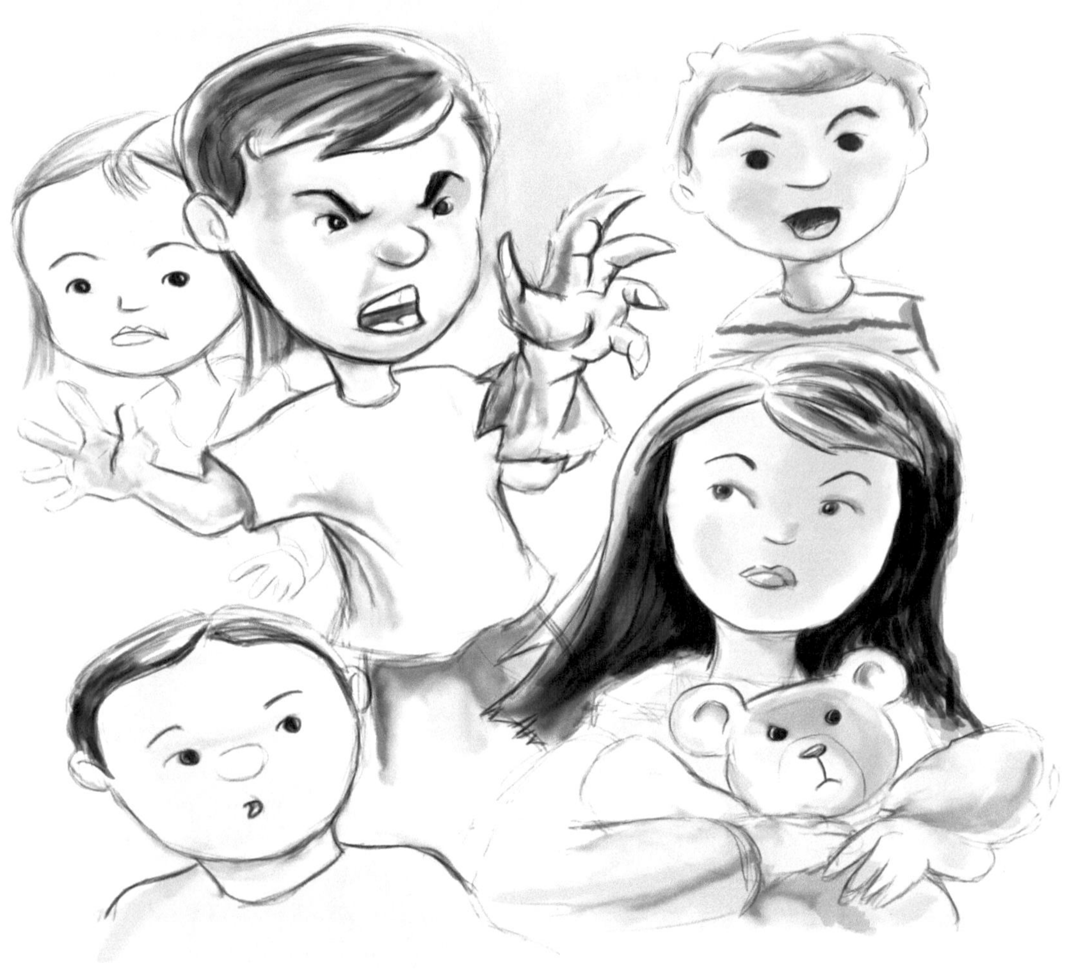

I have never been a fan of black and white art for children's books, however this client wanted his book illustrated in black and white, so…

You always try to do what the customer wants.

I was actually happy about a few of the illustrations.

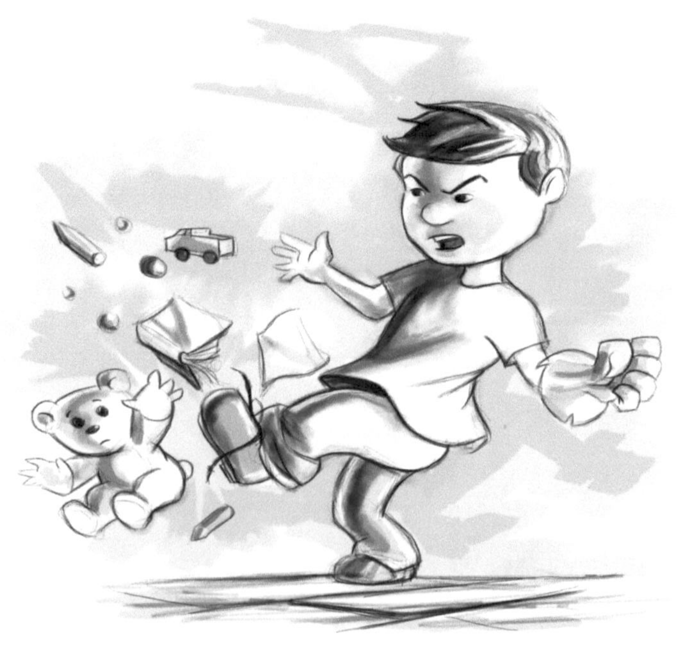

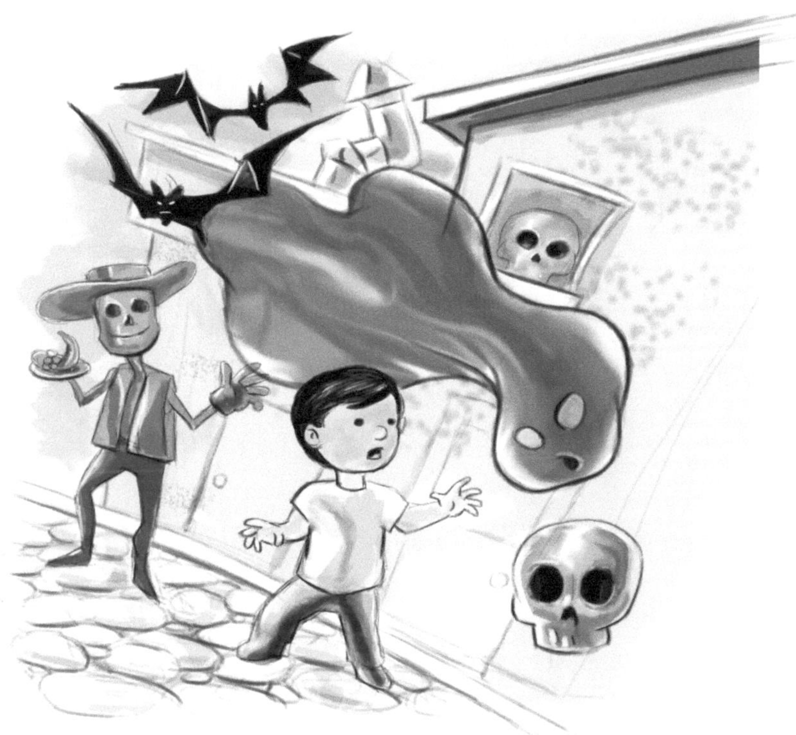

I do not shy away from black and white illustrations, actually I like doing them, and in the right place and subject matter they can be very effective and powerful. However, I feel the more colorful you can be, the better the appeal for children.

It was a challenge for me to do these illustrations and not color them. However, I think that I successfully told the story through the use of creative shading.

This Mariachi Band is my favorite illustration from this project.

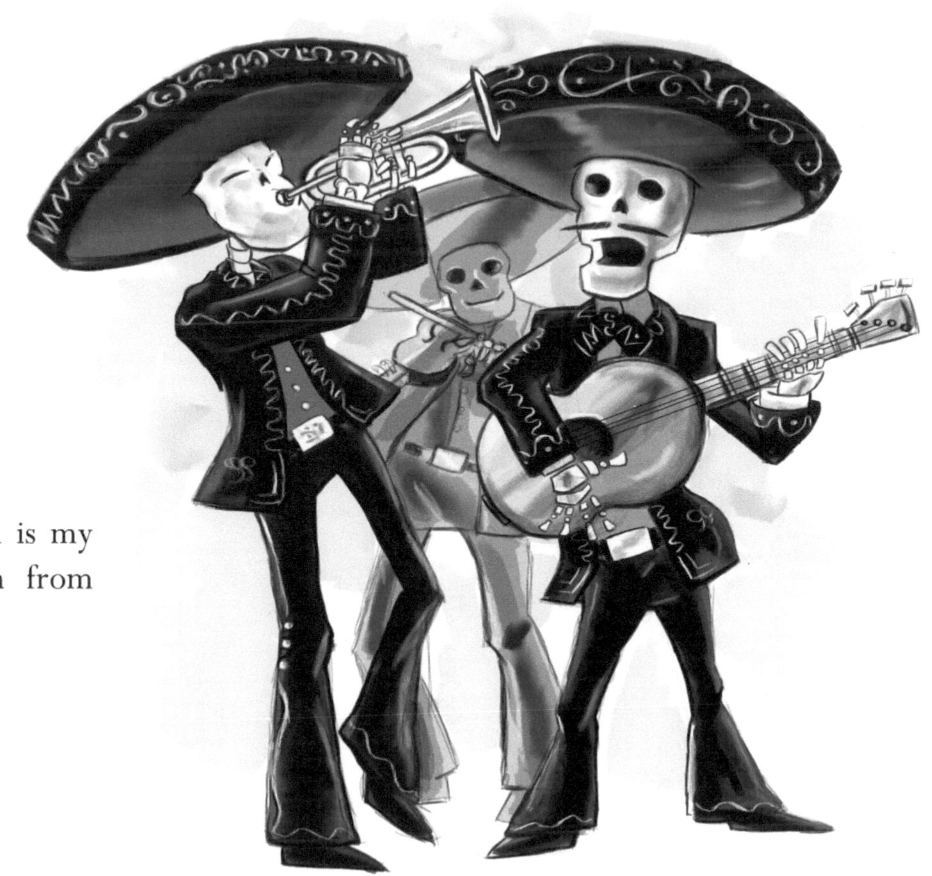

The Kingdom of Clowns -a book
by David Niel Wilson is a story
about his son and his many hats.
Each hat transports him to a
different world- at least in his
imagination.

With these illustrations I tried to
juxtapose the imagination of the
child and let the viewer in on what
the child was seeing in his mind as
he was playing.

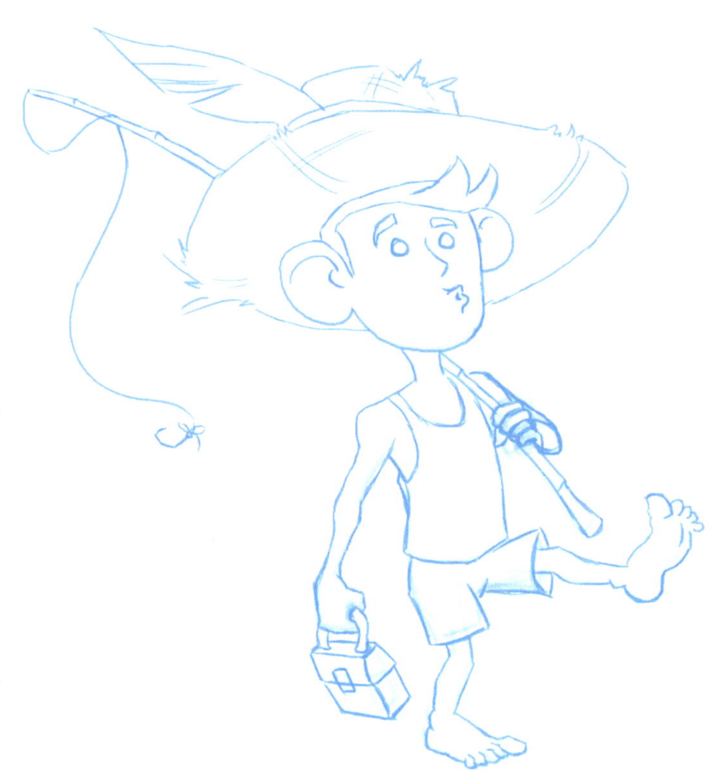

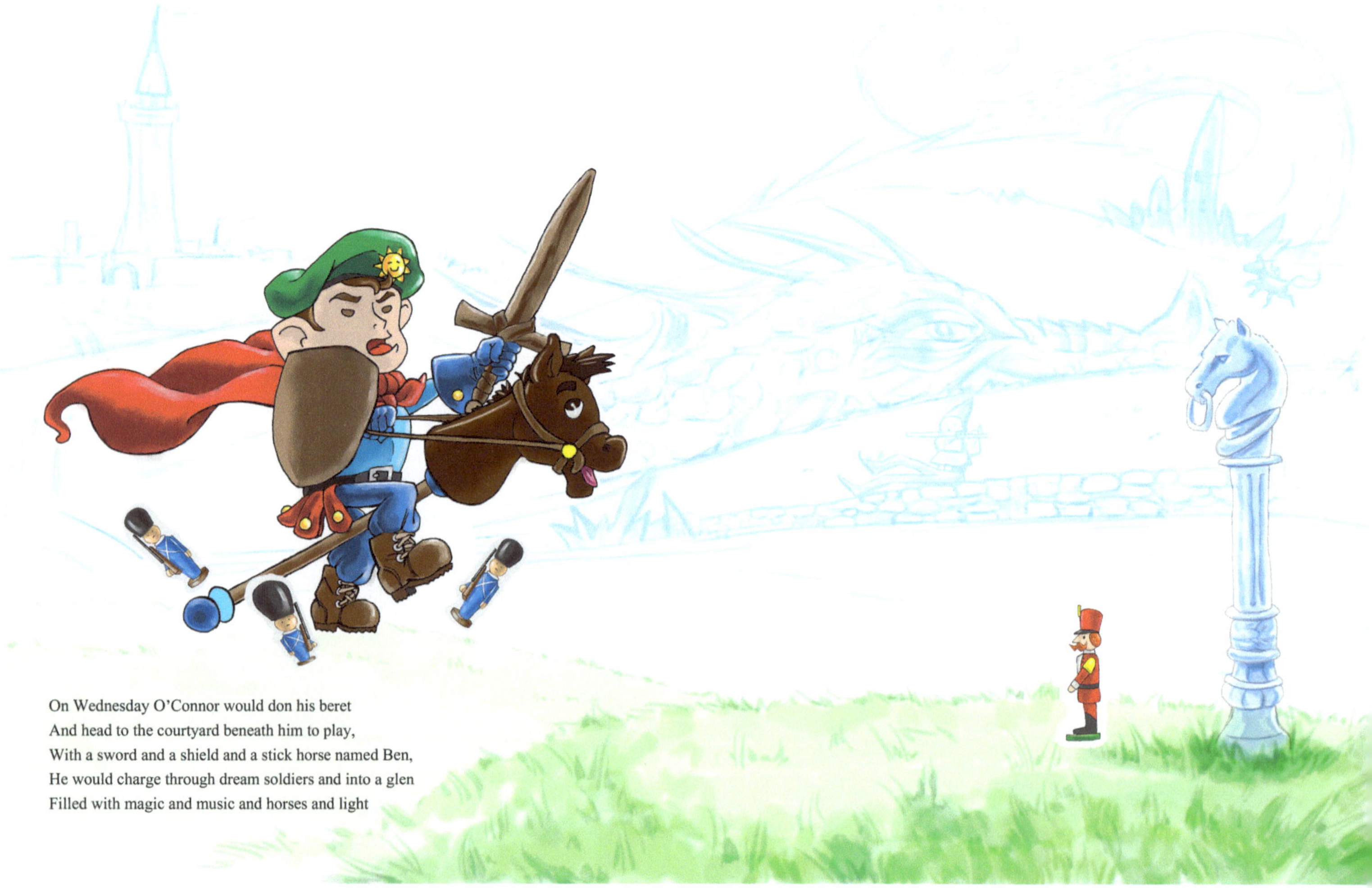

On Wednesday O'Connor would don his beret
And head to the courtyard beneath him to play,
With a sword and a shield and a stick horse named Ben,
He would charge through dream soldiers and into a glen
Filled with magic and music and horses and light

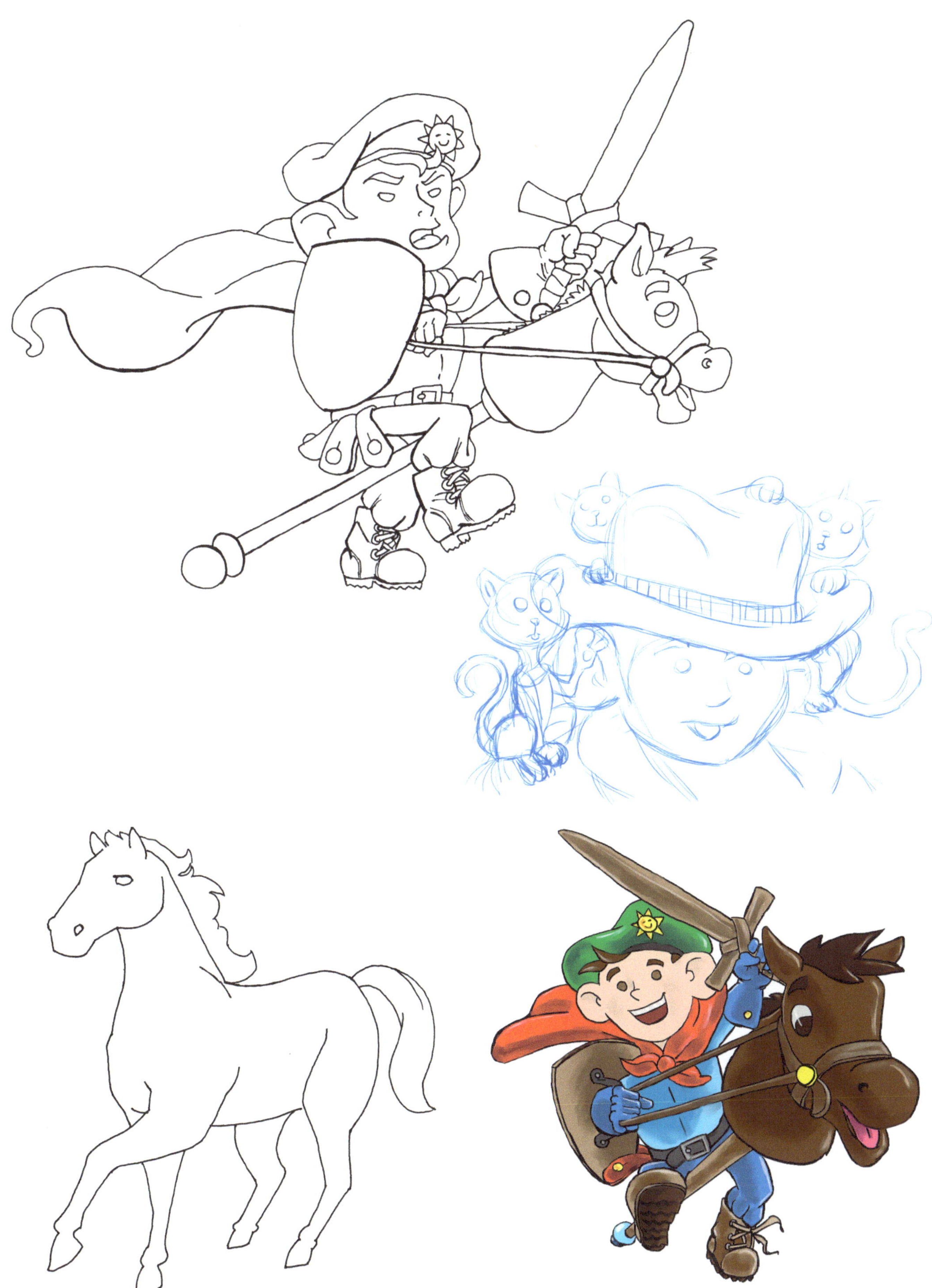

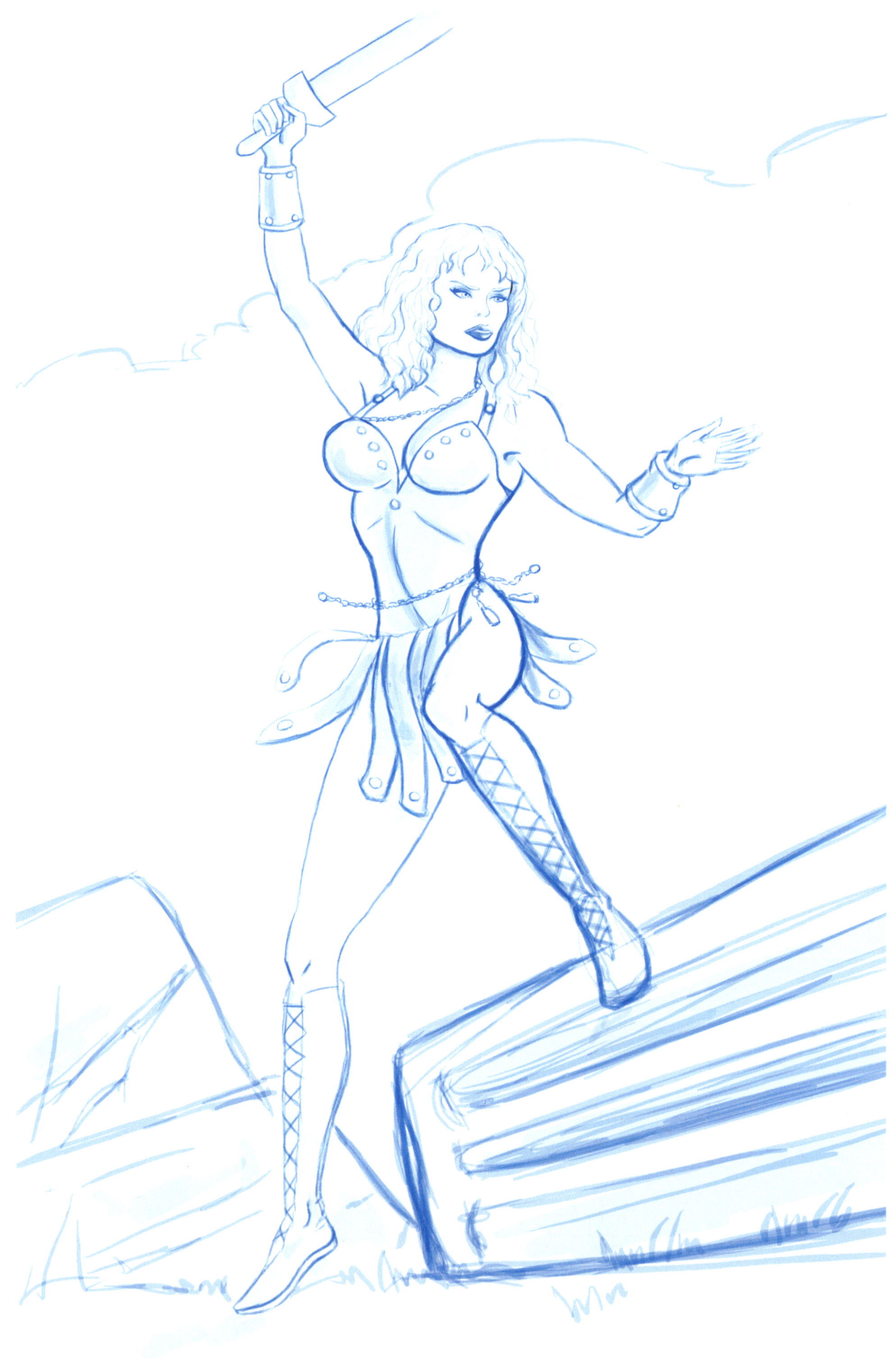

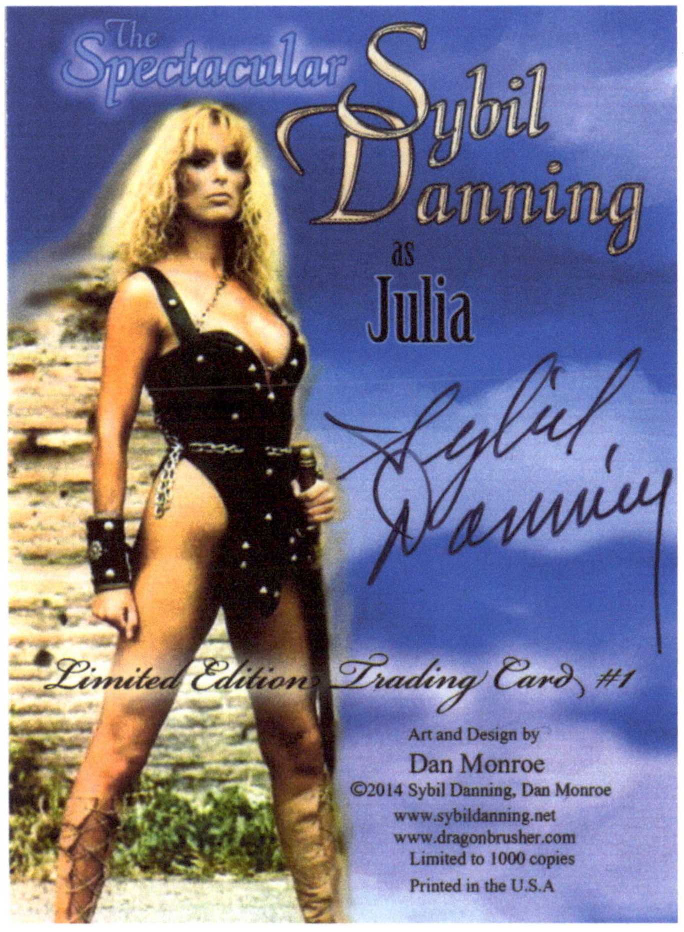

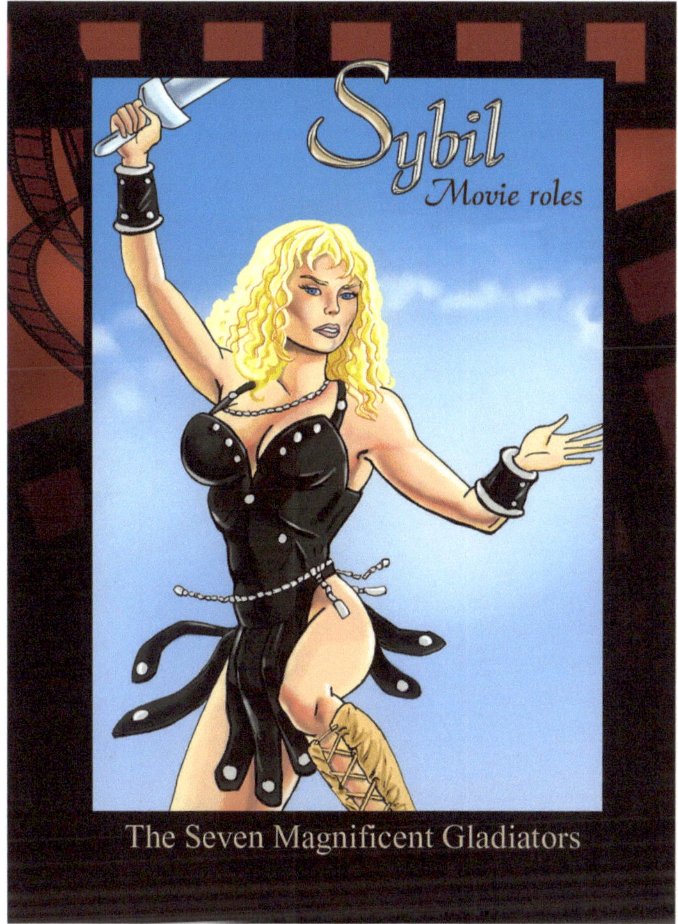

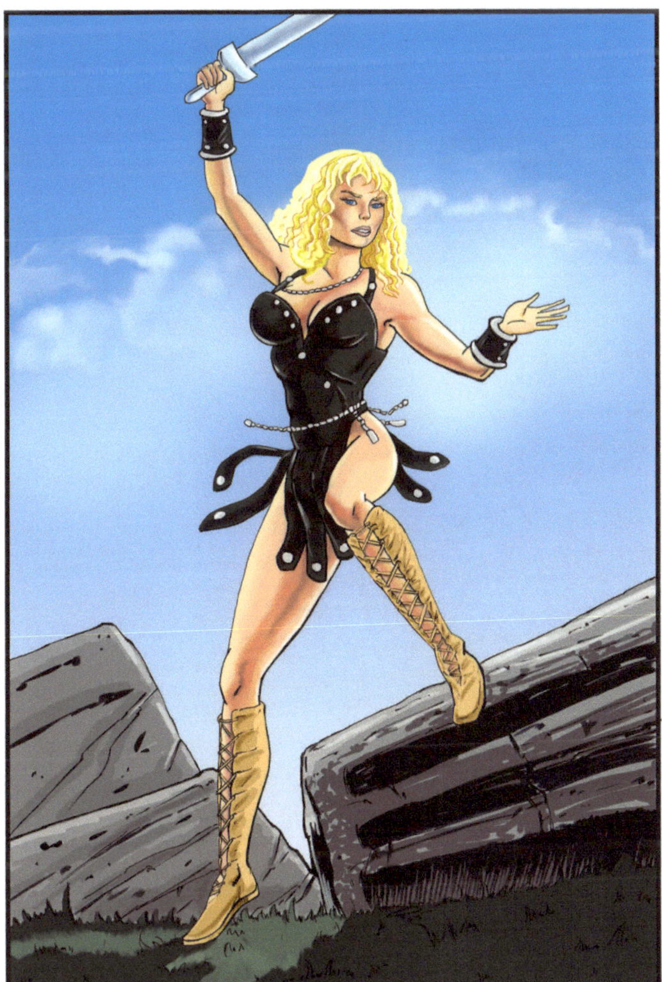

Being a young man in the 1980's, Sybil Danning was always one of my favorite female models who worked in the movies and as a Playboy playmate. She had roles in many movies which attained cult-classic status.

It was a thrill for me to work with her on the creation of this trading card. We spoke on a regular basis during the design process, and her own ideas came through the art as well. She always treated me with respect- a very classy woman.

I designed this as a "signature card" for her to sign and sell when she makes appearances. Each copy of this card is hand signed by her.

I am under contract to do another card with her that I will be designing later this year. I am looking forward to working with her again!

Above shows the front and back of the card.
Left- The entire illustration.

Thor has always been one of my favorite mythical figures of all time. How can any artist not be moved by the imagery of him riding across the skies in a chariot and smashing giant snakes with a his mighty hammer!

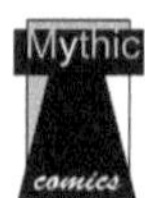

Thor is always electrically charged, so his hair flow's in lightning-like tendrils.

Ye gawds!
THOR

The mighty son of Odin. Thor is the god of thunder and lightening. He is the embodiment of the air element.

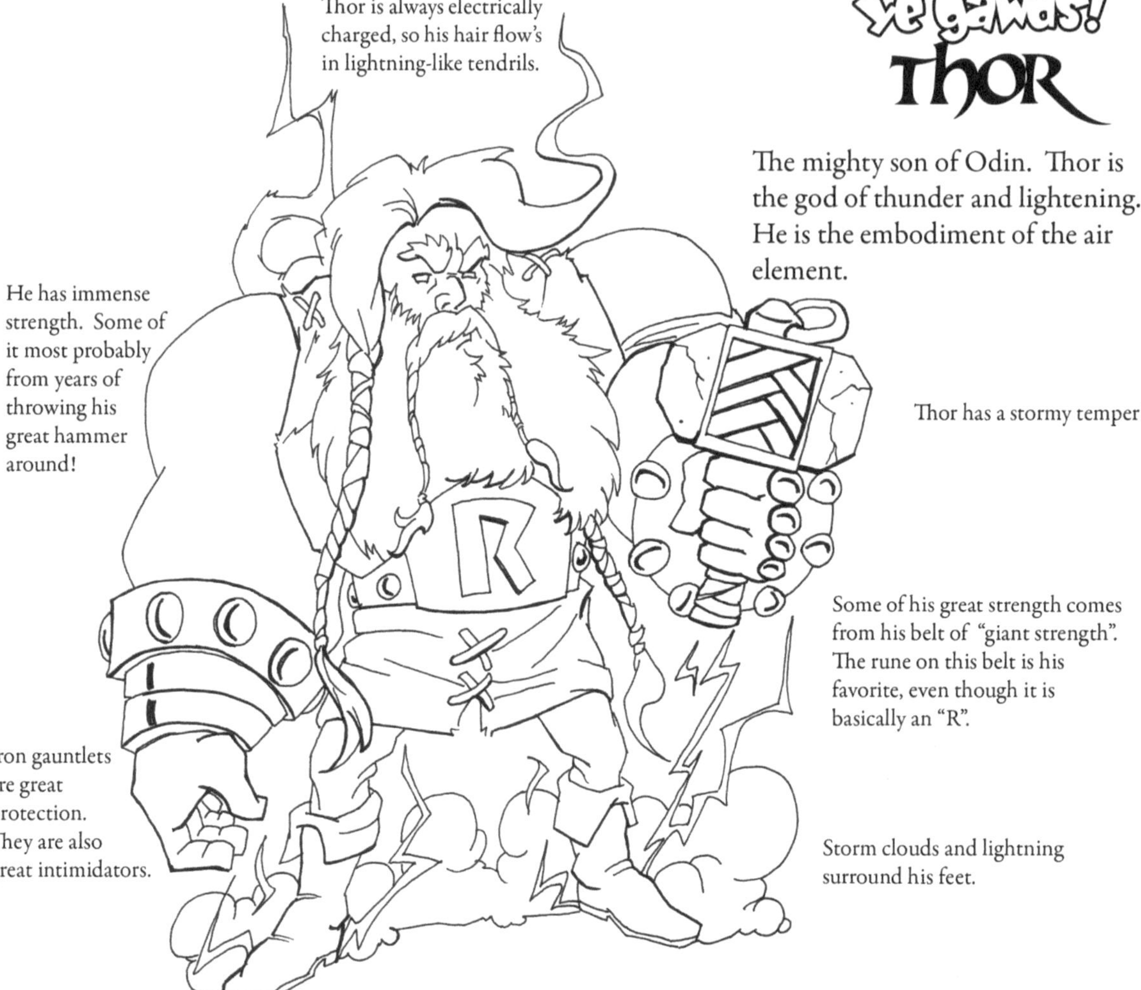

He has immense strength. Some of it most probably from years of throwing his great hammer around!

Thor has a stormy temper!

Some of his great strength comes from his belt of "giant strength". The rune on this belt is his favorite, even though it is basically an "R".

Iron gauntlets are great protection. They are also great intimidators.

Storm clouds and lightning surround his feet.

Mjolnir
The mystic hammer

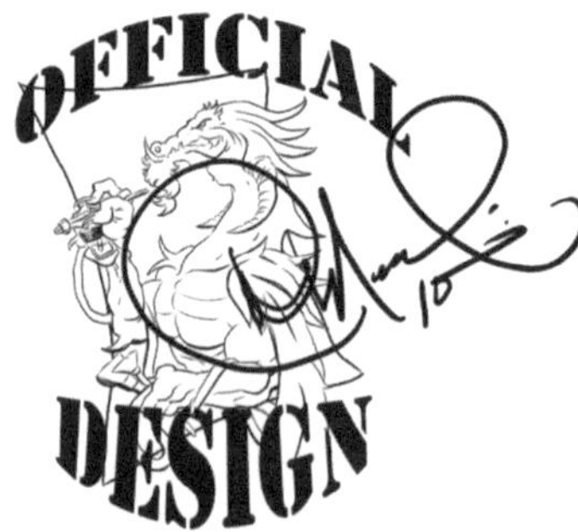

Thor character is an original design by Dan Monroe. © 2009 Dan Monroe

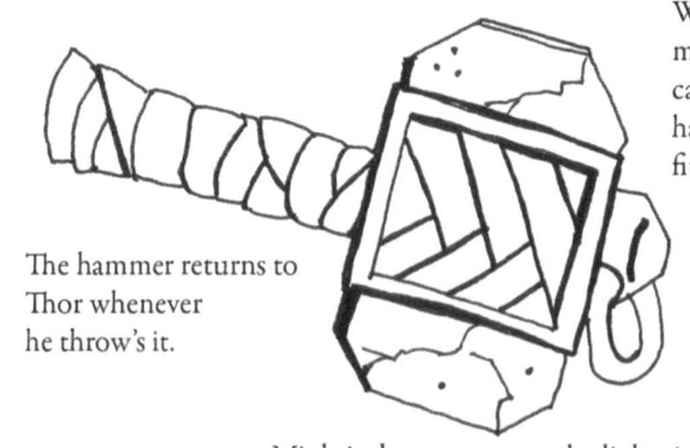

With a single magical word, Thor can shrink the hammer so it will fit into his pocket.

The hammer returns to Thor whenever he throw's it.

Mjolnir does not create the lightning. Thor channels his lightning through the hammer.

Mythic comics

MORRIGAN
goddess of magic

I have chosen this Celtic goddess for several reasons such as her strength and indomitable spirit. She is the original dark queen and so all sorceress and witch characters have been based upon her, even if it was not realized or intentional.

Her tri-colored hair is a nod to the triple-goddess of the ancient cult of the Mothers. Her origin.

She is known by many names; Raven Mistress, the Washerwoman, Queen of the Emerald Isle, are just a few of them.

She has an imperial outlook and comanding prescence. She is not accustomed to being refused.

Her magic is extremely strong. She is also an accomplished shape-shifter.

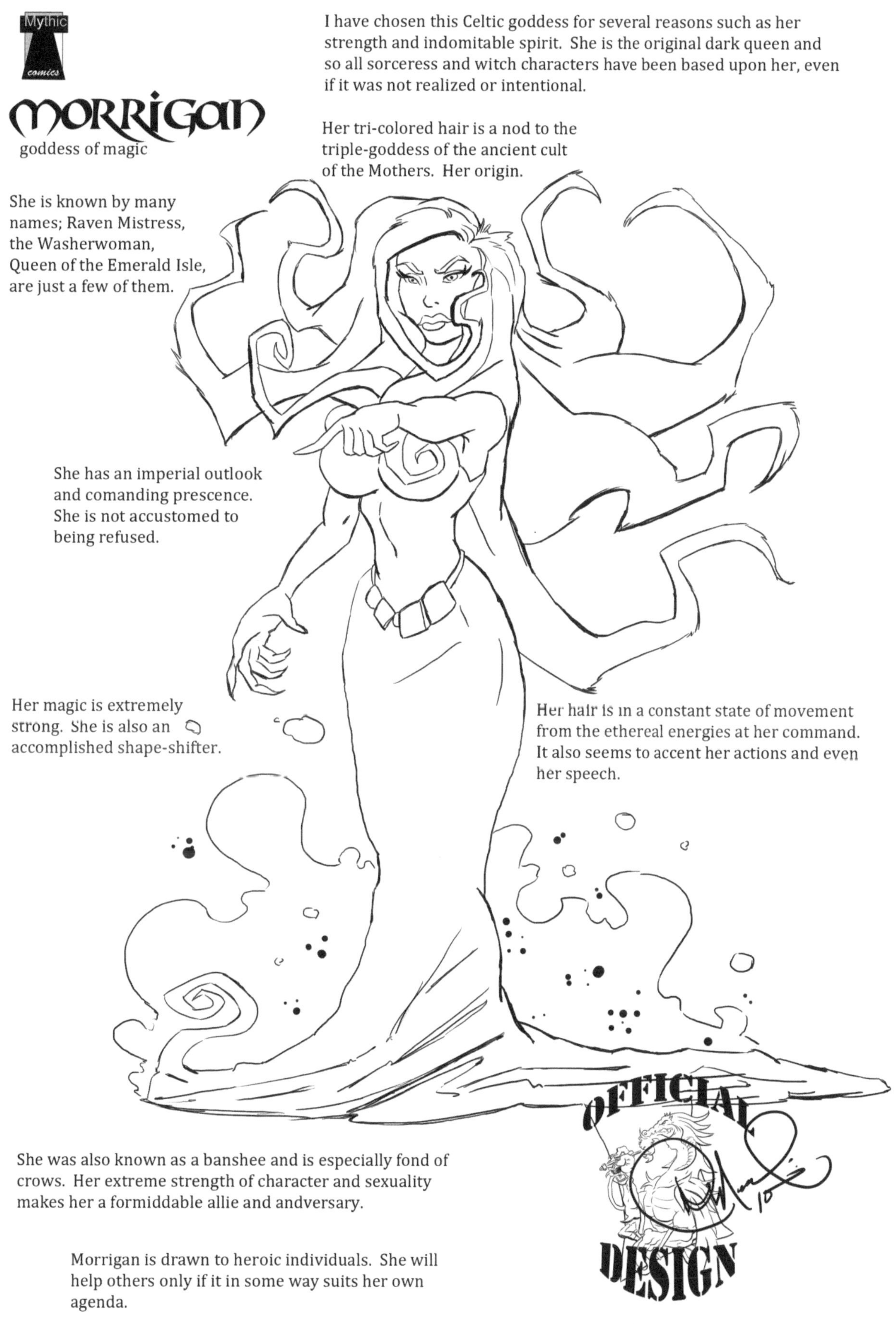

Her hair is in a constant state of movement from the ethereal energies at her command. It also seems to accent her actions and even her speech.

She was also known as a banshee and is especially fond of crows. Her extreme strength of character and sexuality makes her a formiddable allie and andversary.

Morrigan is drawn to heroic individuals. She will help others only if it in some way suits her own agenda.

Thor character is an original design by Dan Monroe. © 2009 Dan Monroe

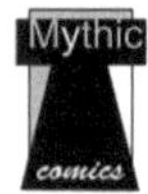

Ye gawds!
Hercules

The son of Zeus. He is the embodiment of the earth element. He is a demi-god. Hercules often has trouble controlling his mega-god strength which gets him into trouble.

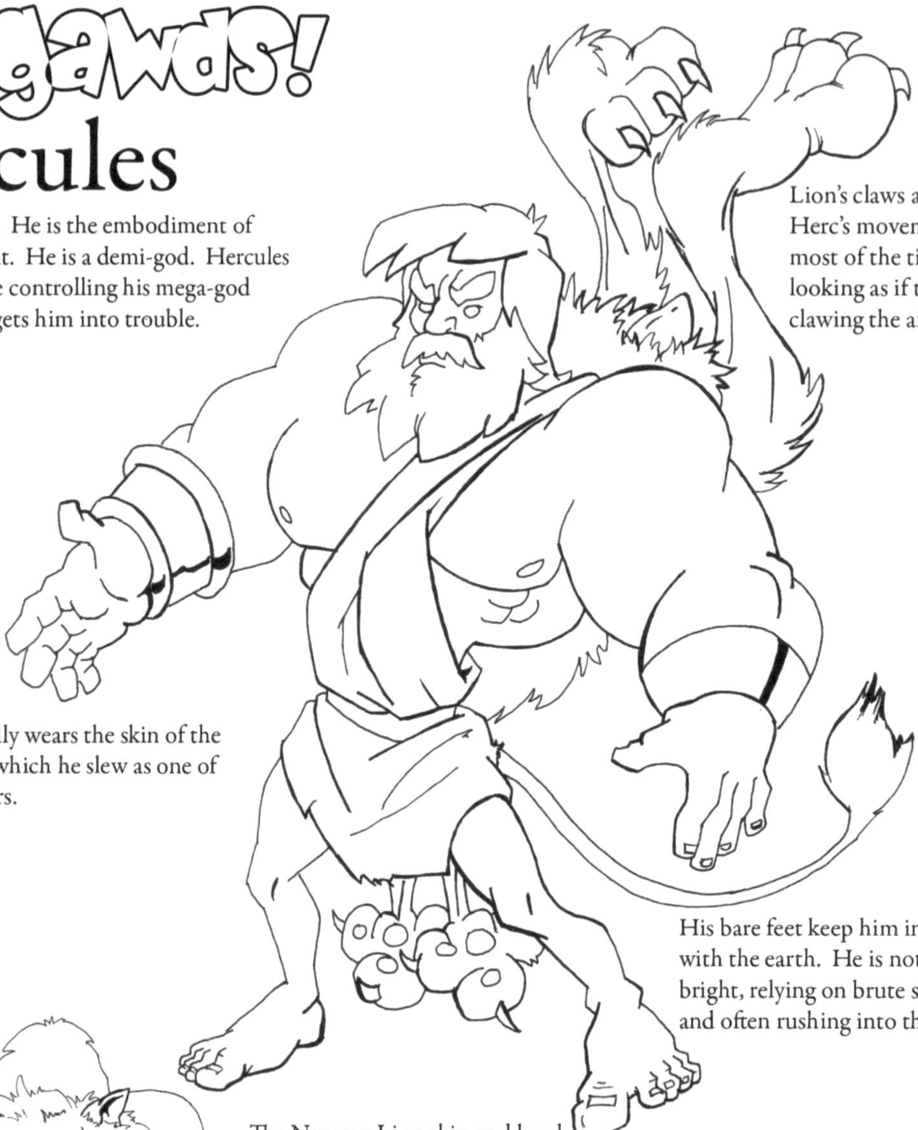

Hercules is another of my favorite mythical characters, the fact that he is nearly unequaled in natural strength. Natural in the idea that it is his birthright and not enhanced by any magical means.

Lion's claws accent Herc's movements, most of the time looking as if they are clawing the air!

Hercules actually wears the skin of the Nemean Lion which he slew as one of his twelve labors.

His bare feet keep him in touch with the earth. He is not too bright, relying on brute strength and often rushing into the fight.

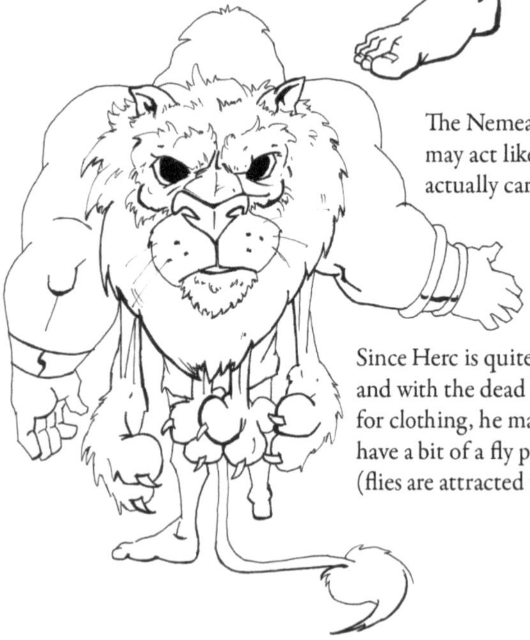

The Nemean Lion skin and head may act like a "backpack". He may actually carry things in there.

Since Herc is quite "earthy" and with the dead lion skin for clothing, he may actually have a bit of a fly problem (flies are attracted to him).

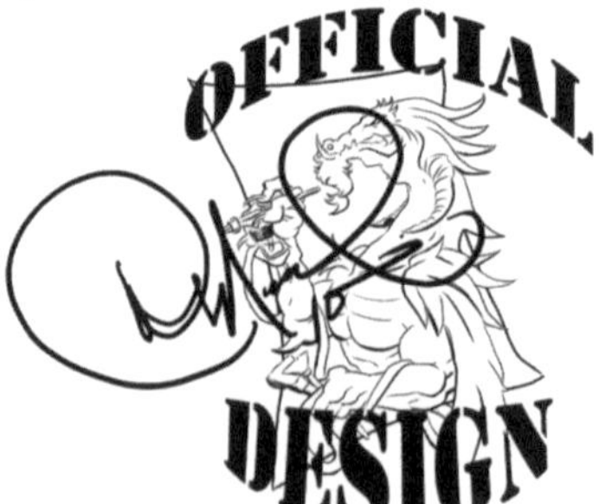

Hercules character is an original design by Dan Monroe. © 2009 Dan Monroe

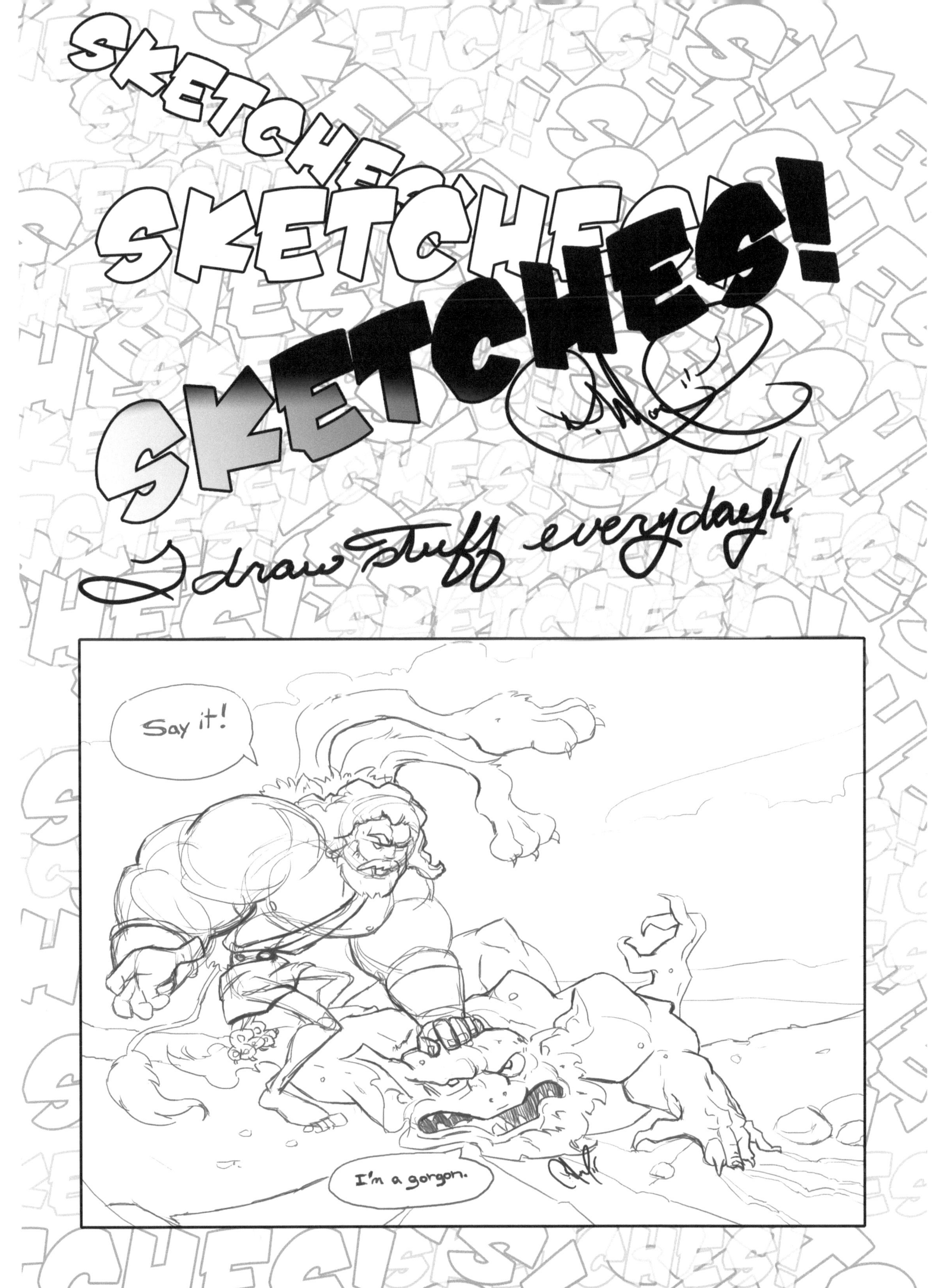
SKETCHES!
SKETCHES!
SKETCHES!
I draw stuff everyday!
Say it!
I'm a gorgon.

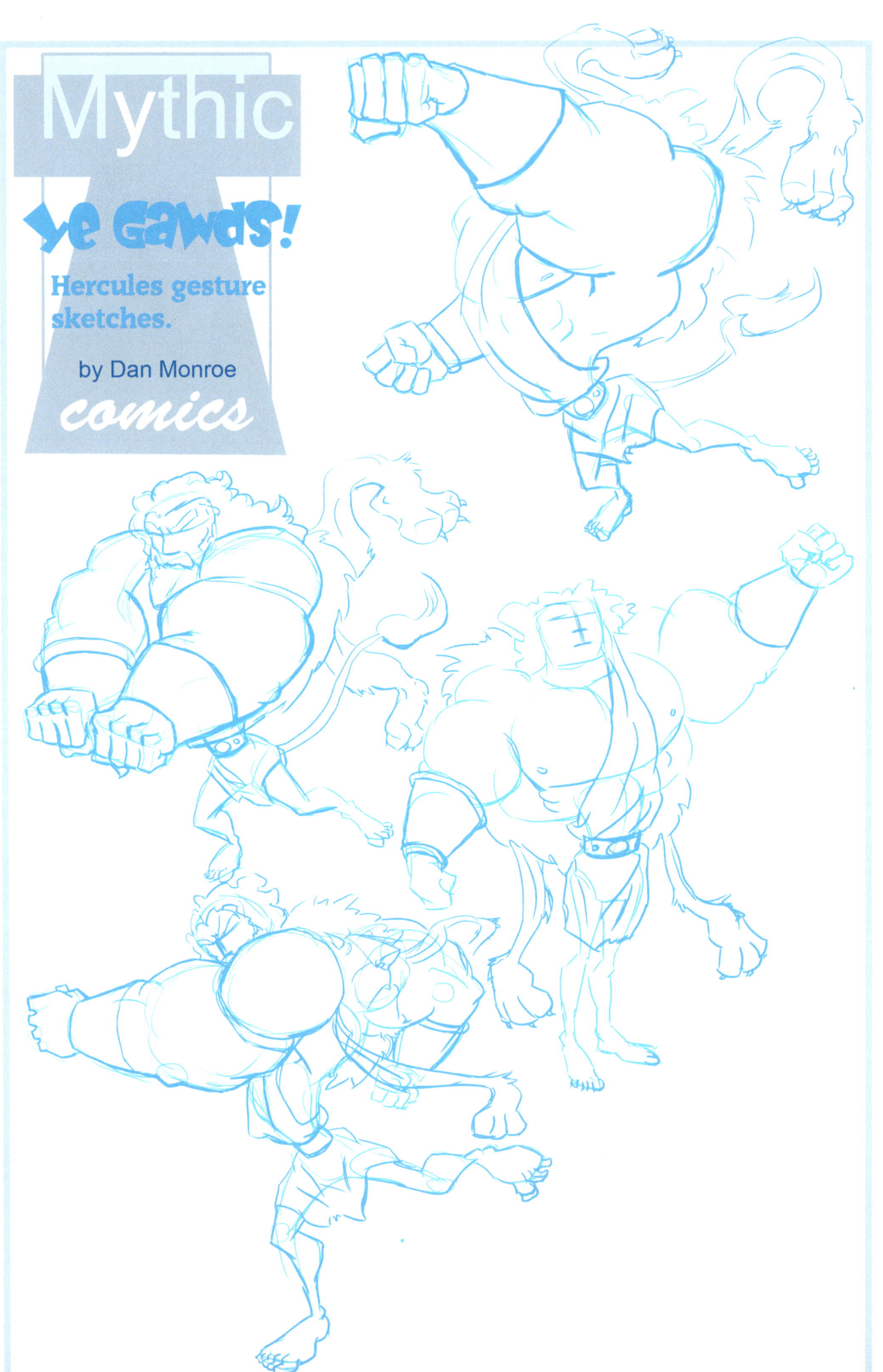

Mythic
ye gawds!
Hercules gesture sketches.
by Dan Monroe
comics

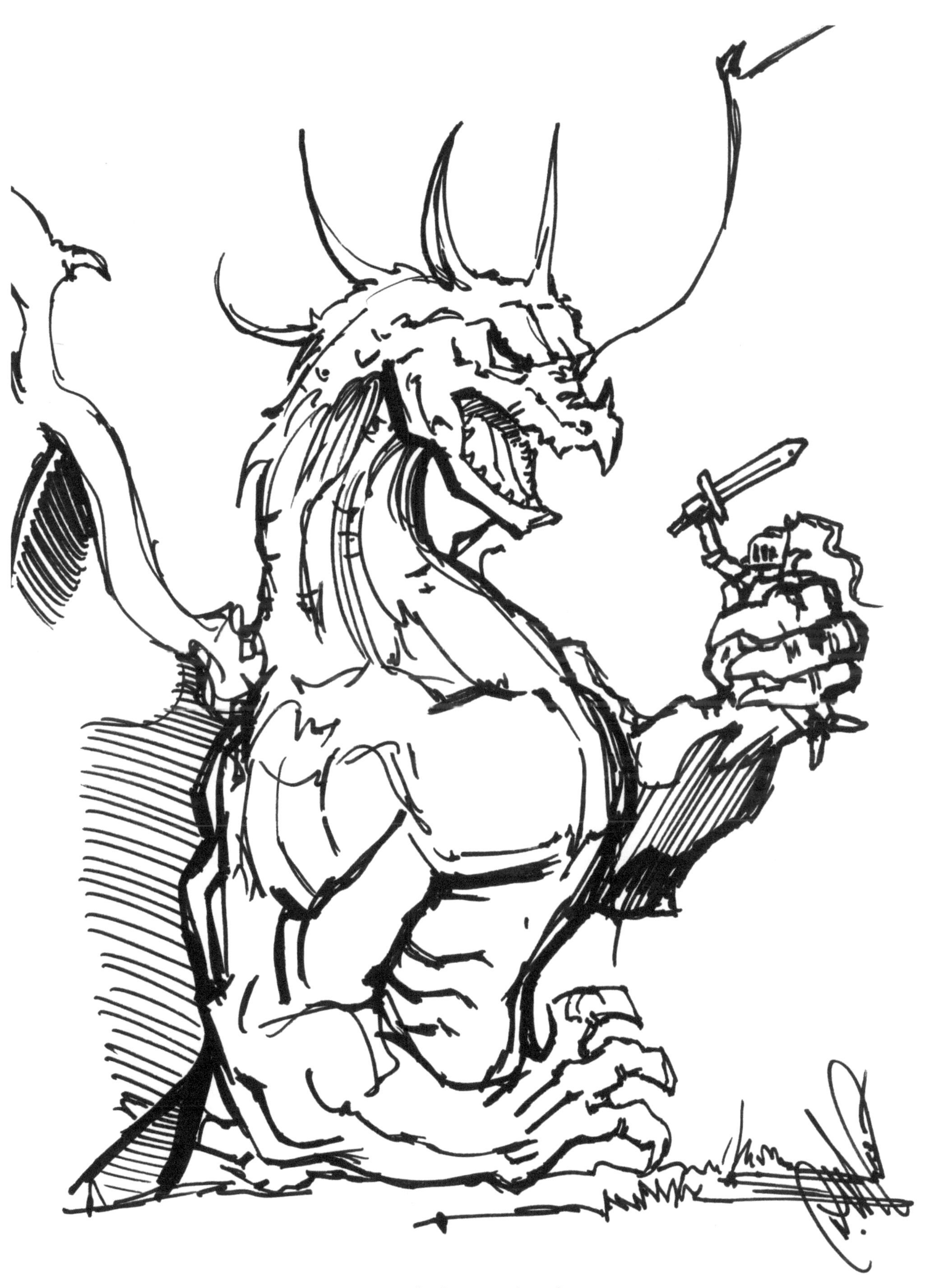

A quick sharpie sketch.

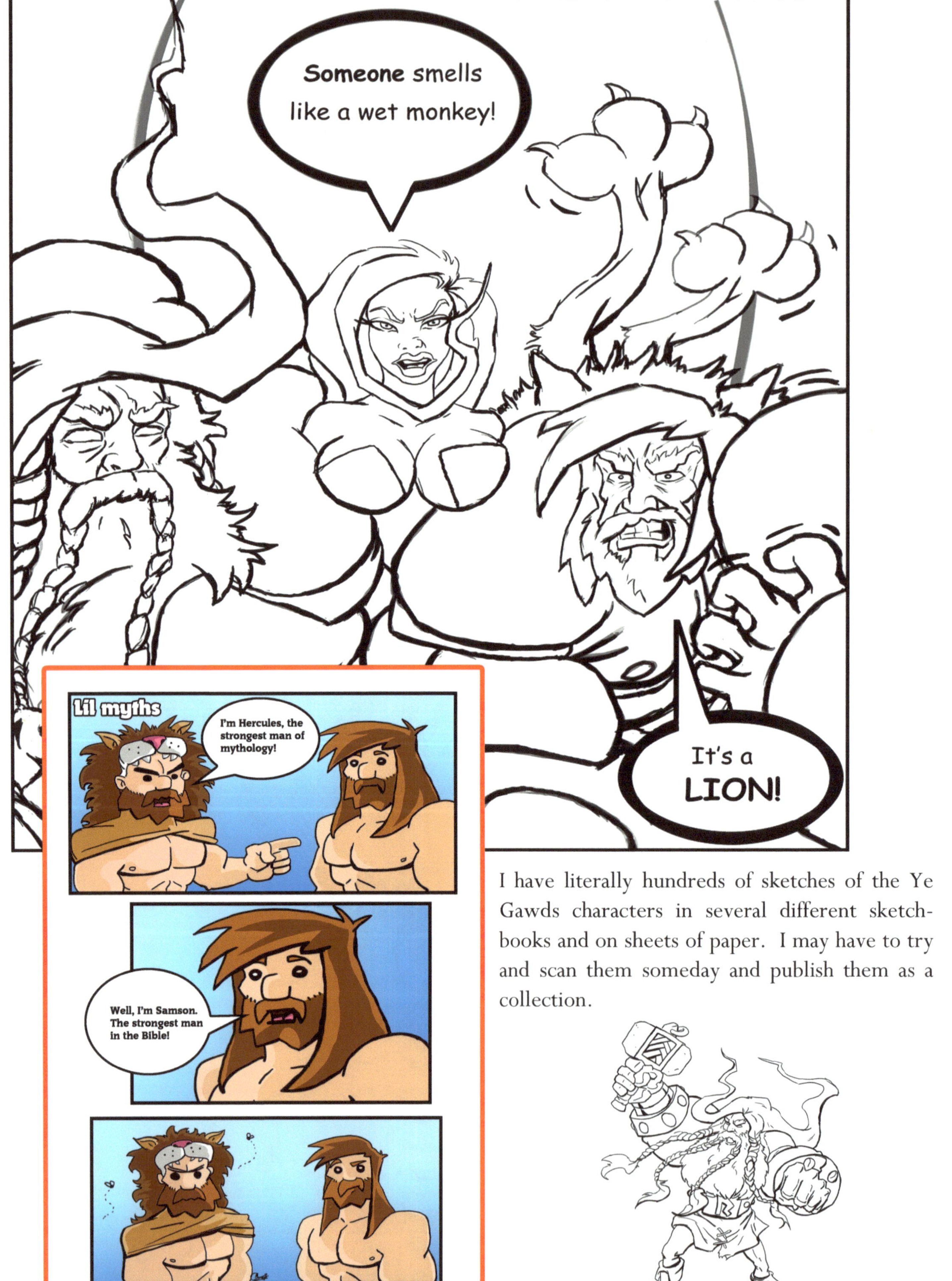

I have literally hundreds of sketches of the Ye Gawds characters in several different sketch-books and on sheets of paper. I may have to try and scan them someday and publish them as a collection.

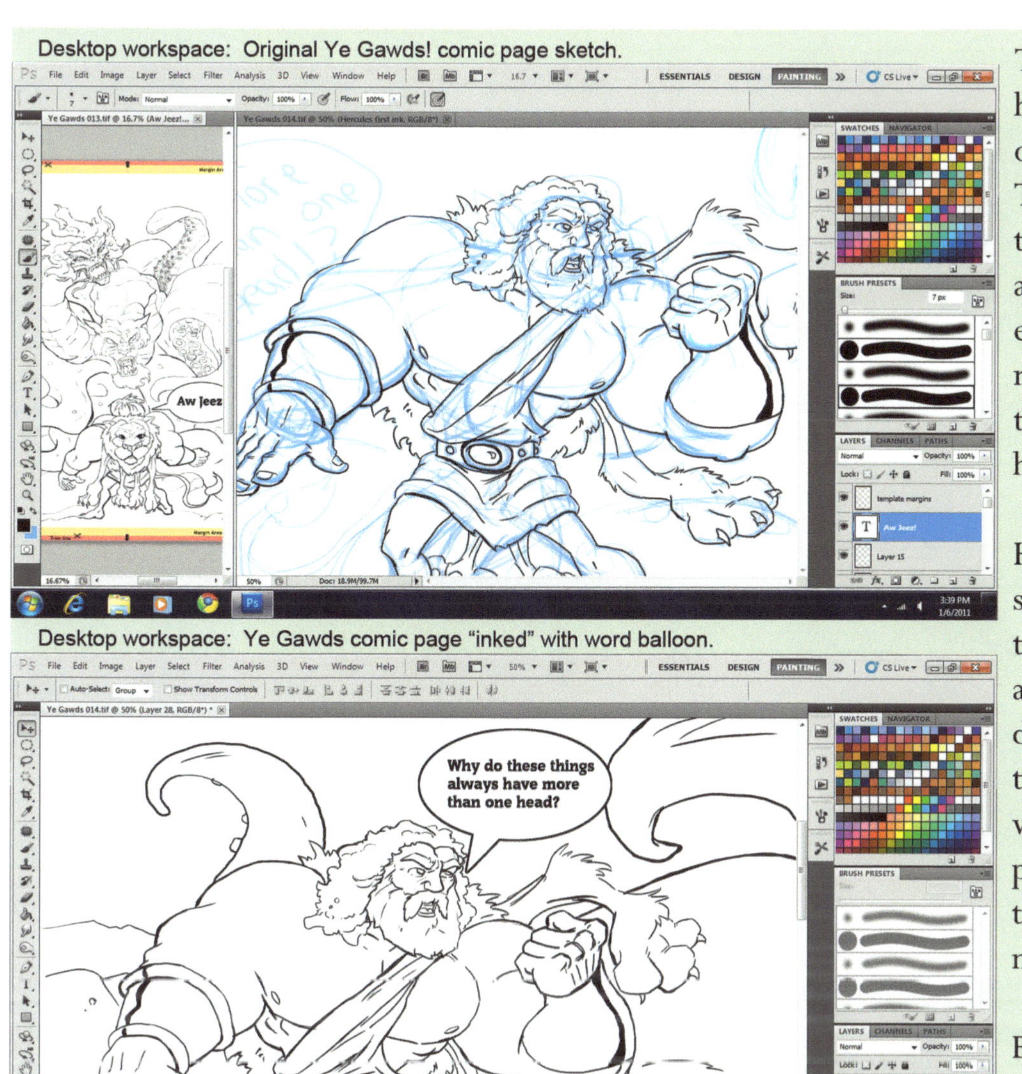

Desktop workspace: Original Ye Gawds! comic page sketch.

Desktop workspace: Ye Gawds comic page "inked" with word balloon.

The Ye Gawds characters have always been my favorite original character creations. They have a certain freedom to them as far as how they act and how I draw them which is extremely enjoyable to me. I return to them as often as time allows- though to be honest, it is not often enough.

Here are a couple of screen-shots of the process I use at times. Sketching in blueline and then wireframing in black digital "ink." I have since re-turned to doing my inkwork with brush and pens and dip-ping ink because the quality of the ink is much better- as are my lines.

Below is a "Commercial" for the trio as TRON-asized ver-sions of themselves.

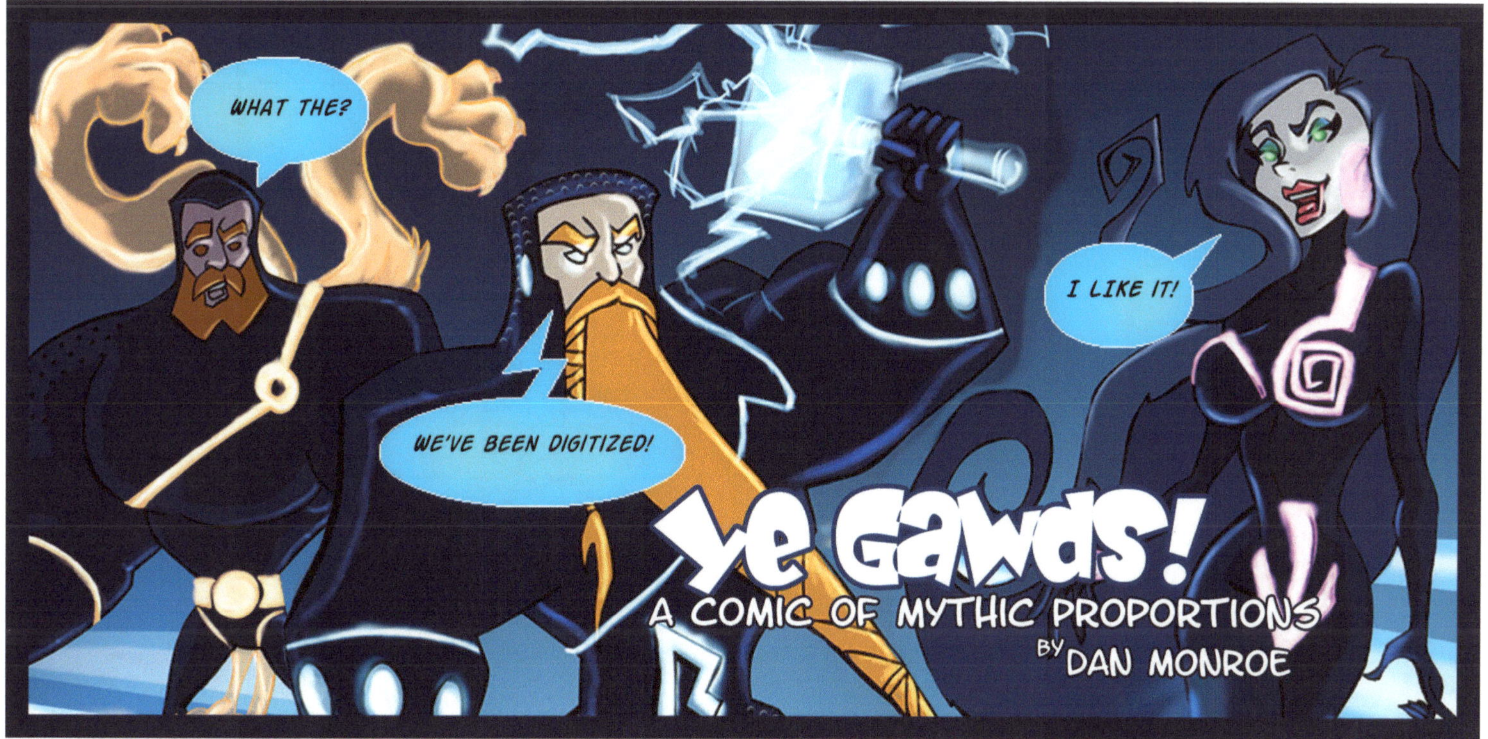

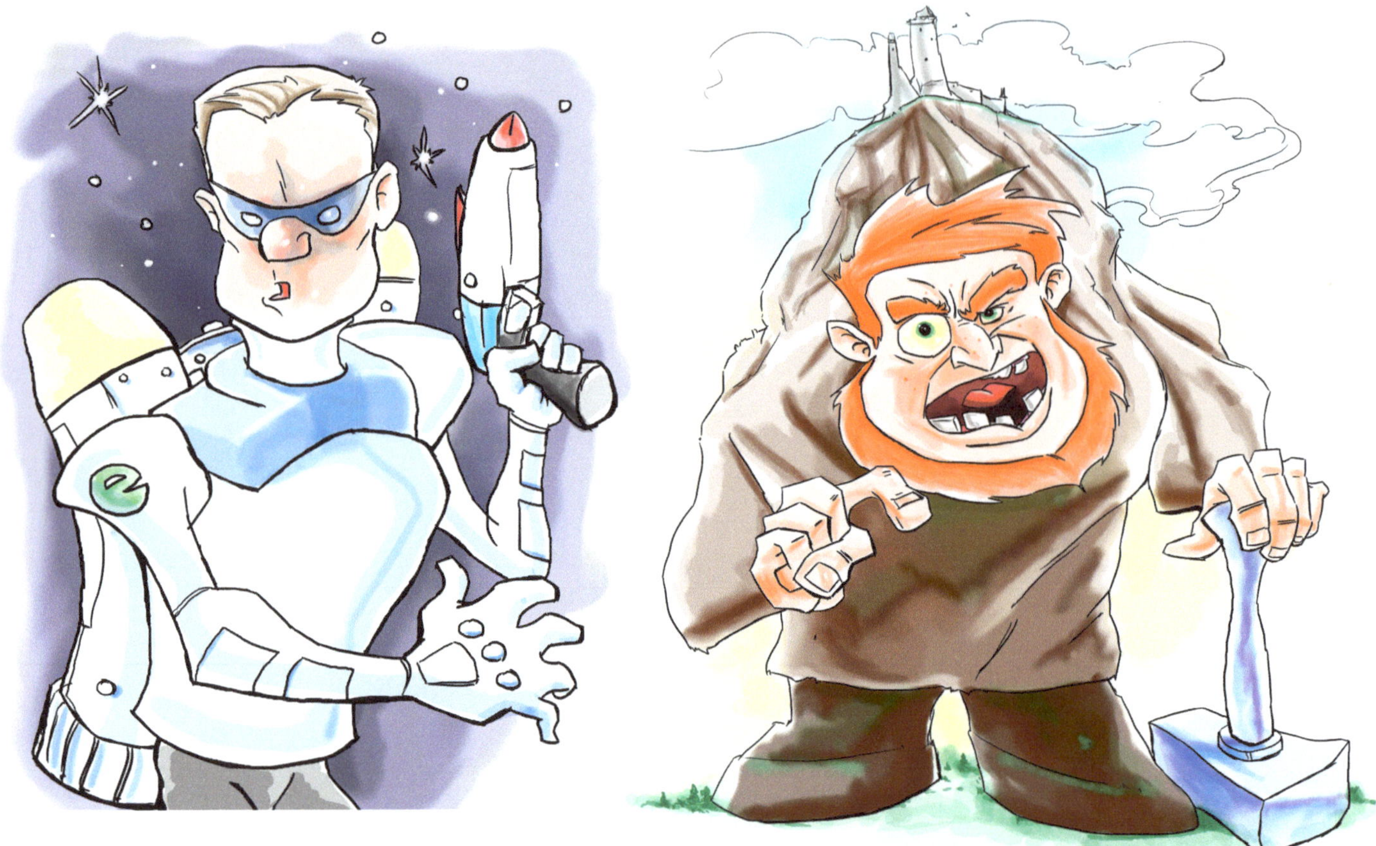

One of my best assets has been my boundless imagination. I find that I can travel between countless dimensions with my artwork.

I try to give every character that I draw, their own personalities, and even in a quick concept such as the ones on this page and the following pages, they should each be able to tell some sort of a story. I am sure that just by looking at them, you would be able to tell me what their stories may be.

That is what illustrators do, we tell stories with our drawings. The actual written text is just there to lend the voice. Stories can easily be told without a word ever being written, at times.

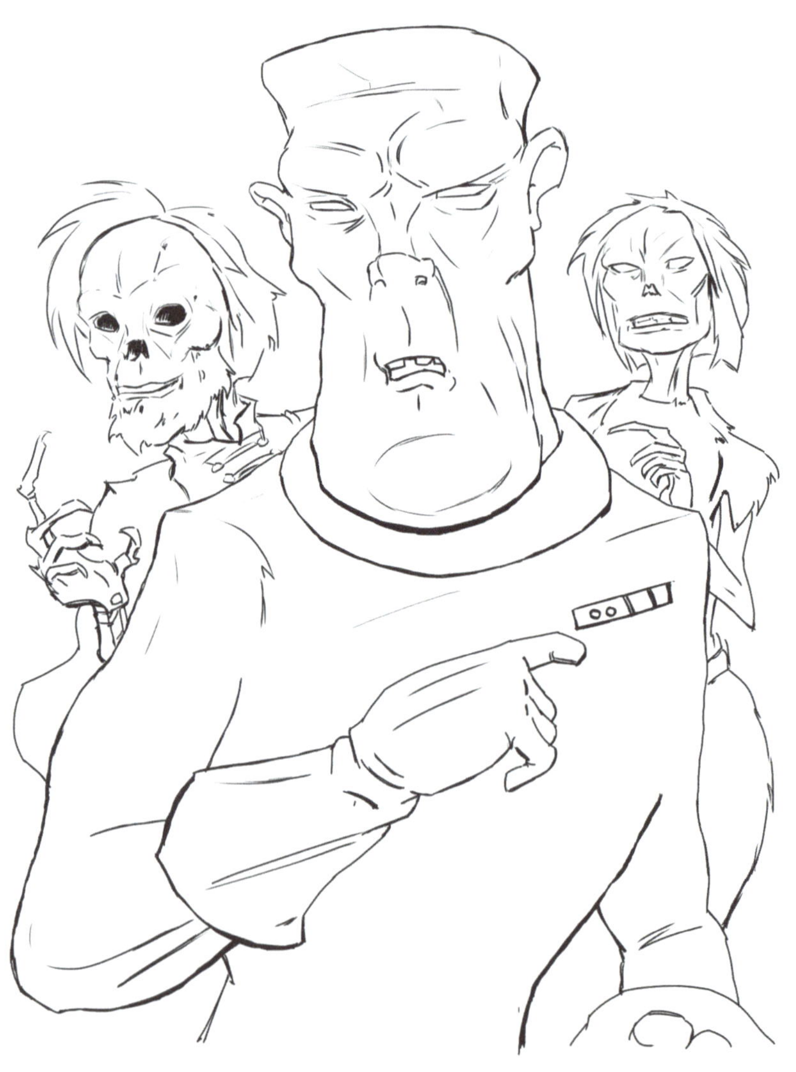

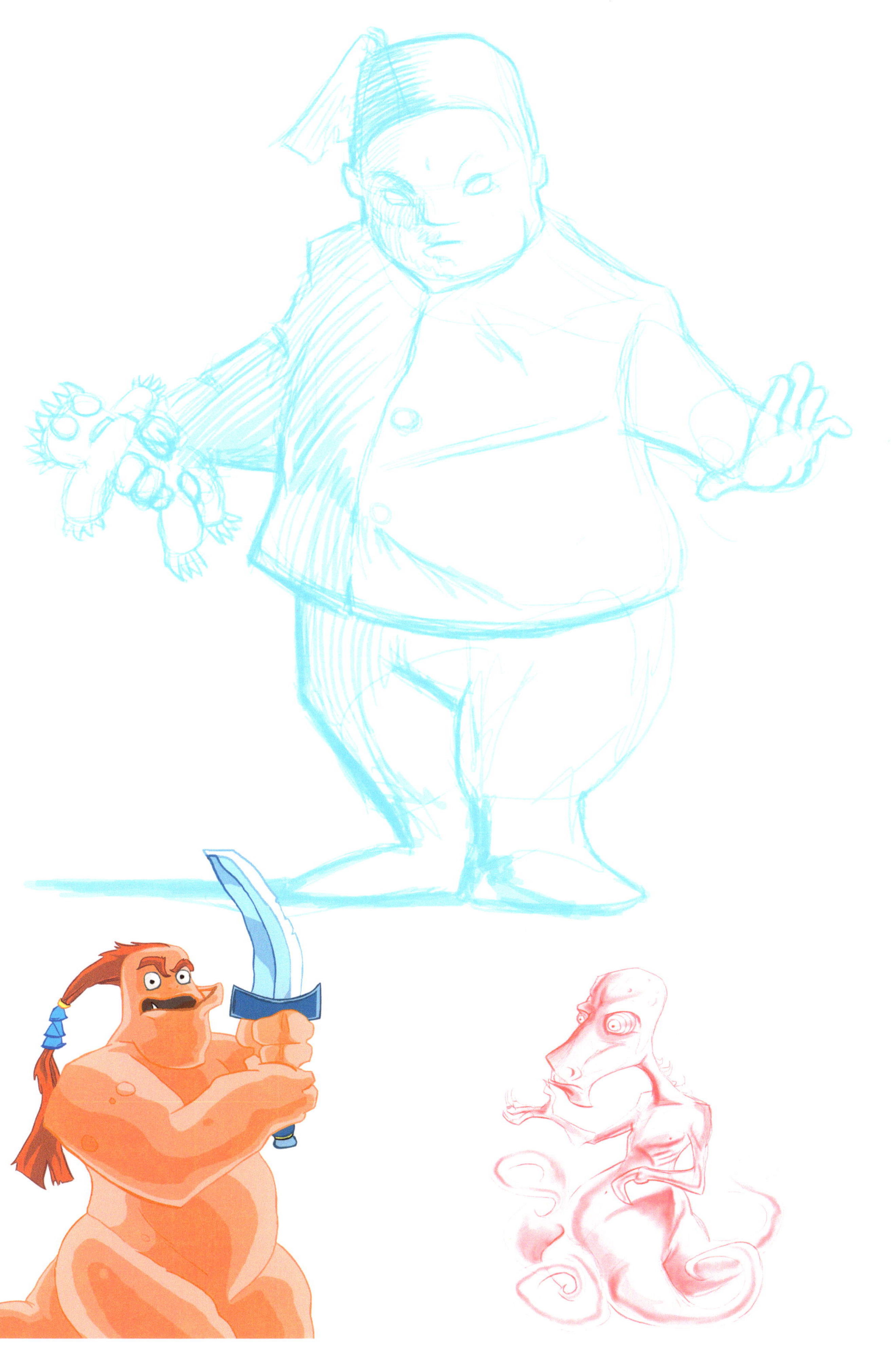

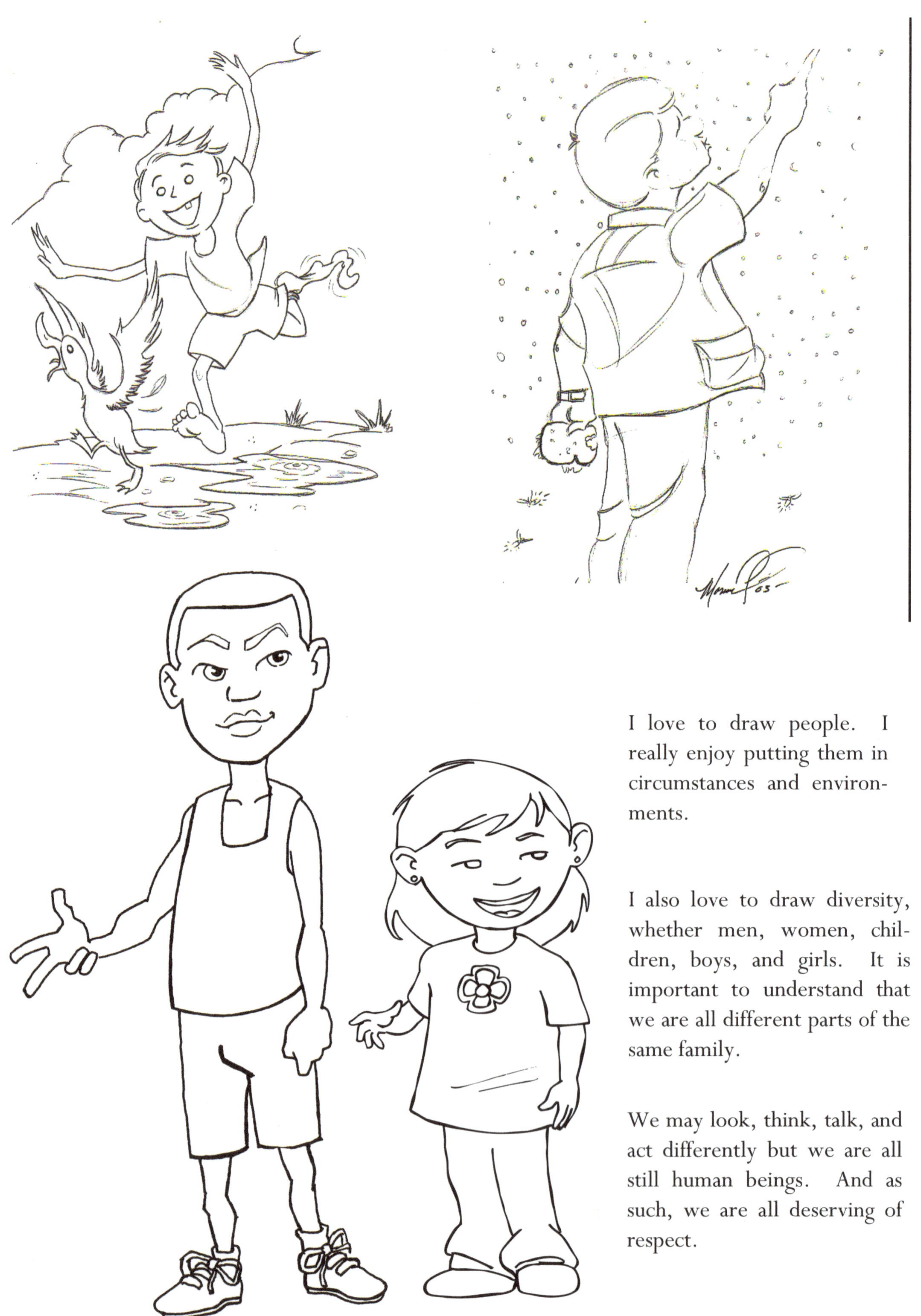

I love to draw people. I really enjoy putting them in circumstances and environments.

I also love to draw diversity, whether men, women, children, boys, and girls. It is important to understand that we are all different parts of the same family.

We may look, think, talk, and act differently but we are all still human beings. And as such, we are all deserving of respect.

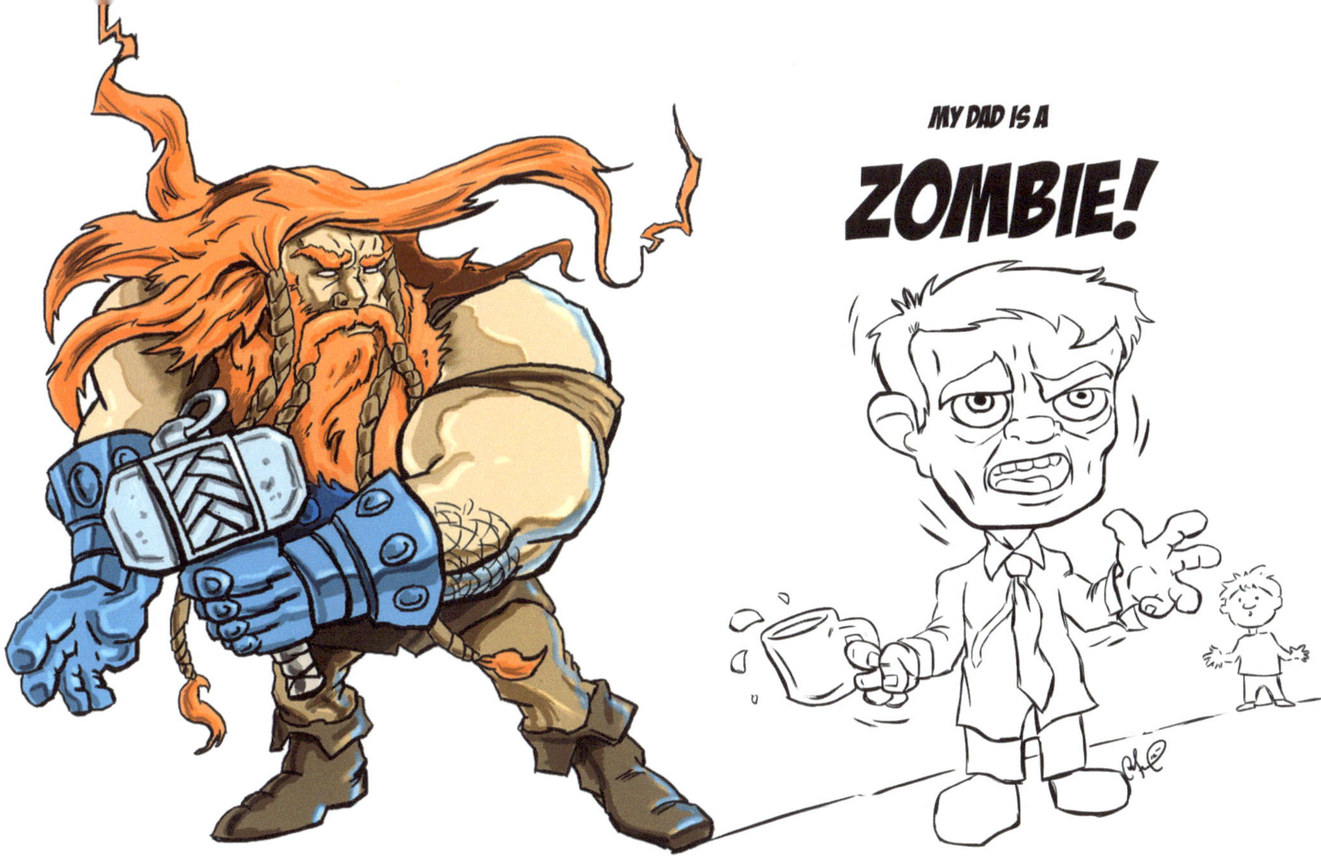

MY DAD IS A
ZOMBIE!

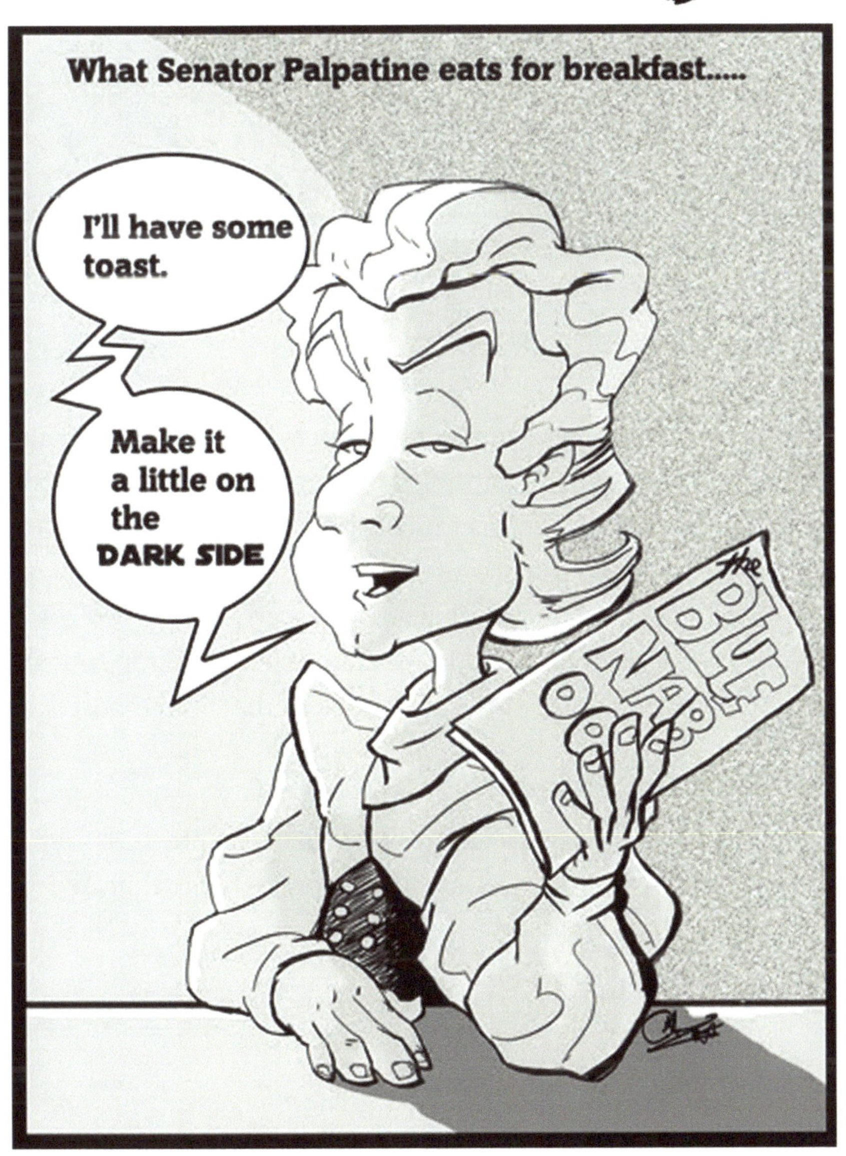

What Senator Palpatine eats for breakfast.....
I'll have some toast.
Make it a little on the DARK SIDE

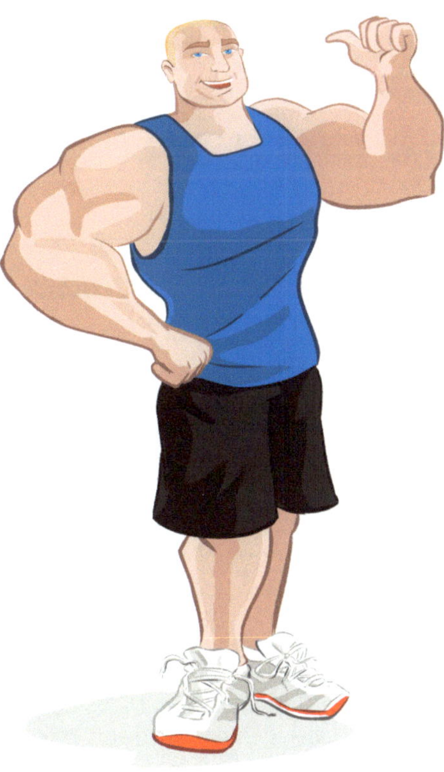

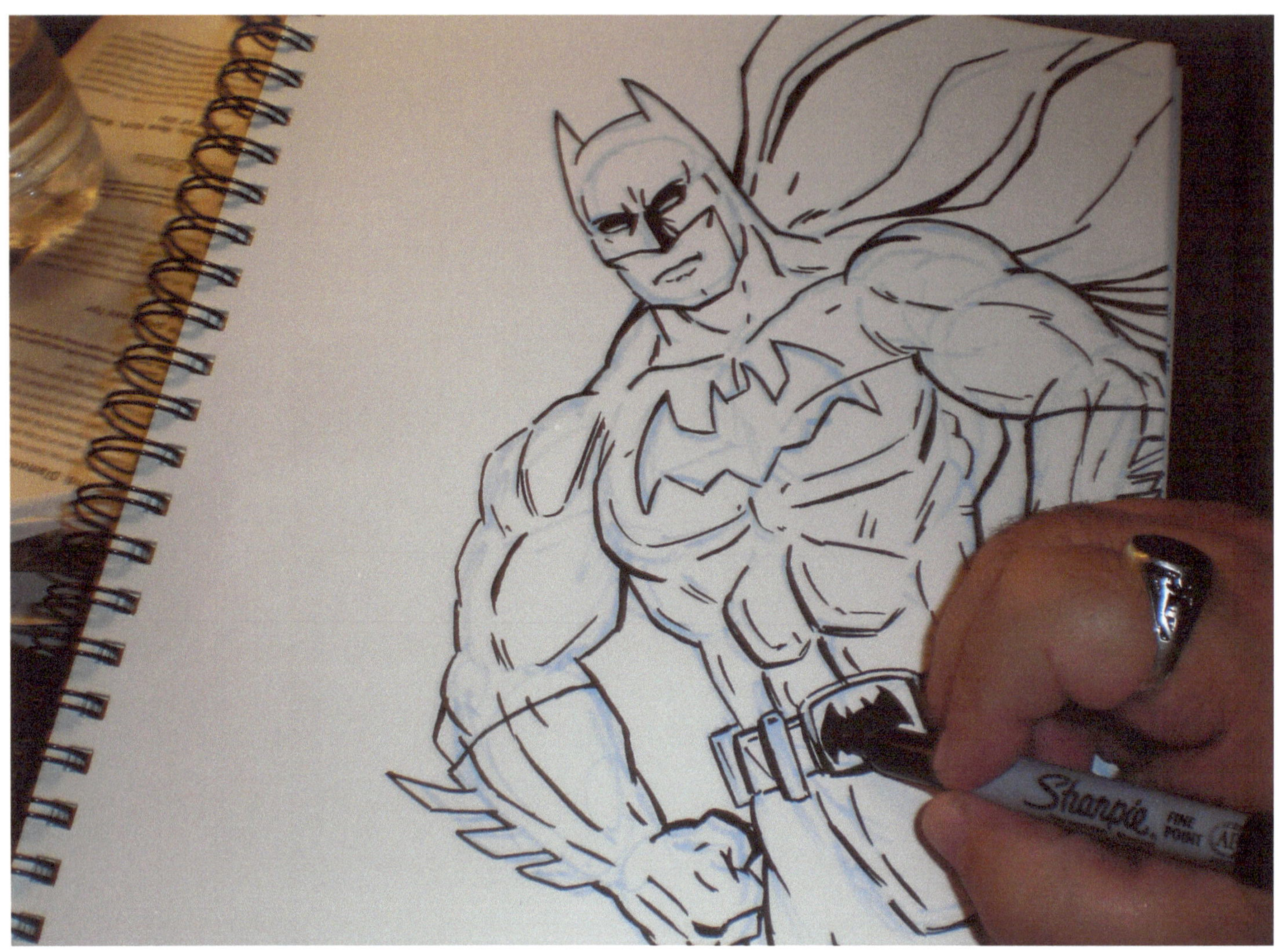

In conclusion-

I know that all the young aspiring artists seem lured to doing so much computer-generated art. There is nothing wrong with that, I do much on the computer as well. The thing to remember however, is that in order to properly use the tools contained within the computer, you must first learn how to actually use the tools as they exist in the real tactile world. Go out and draw on real paper, sketch with real pencils, paint on real canvas, spray paint through real airbrushes- A lot! For once you learn how to use the real tools, and are adept, then you may progress on to the computer and appreciate the art making tool that it is. Always return to the tactile tools, using computer and traditional tools together is the best way to show how well-rounded you are as an artist.

But that is just the humble opinion of this particular guy- me, who has lived much of my life with my hands covered in charcoal dust, or my arms covered in paint up to my elbows. I have probably digested more oil paint and inks than a human probably should, and I have loved every single minute of it! Creating art excites me, I never grow tired of it- and I hope you never do either.

End (for now)...

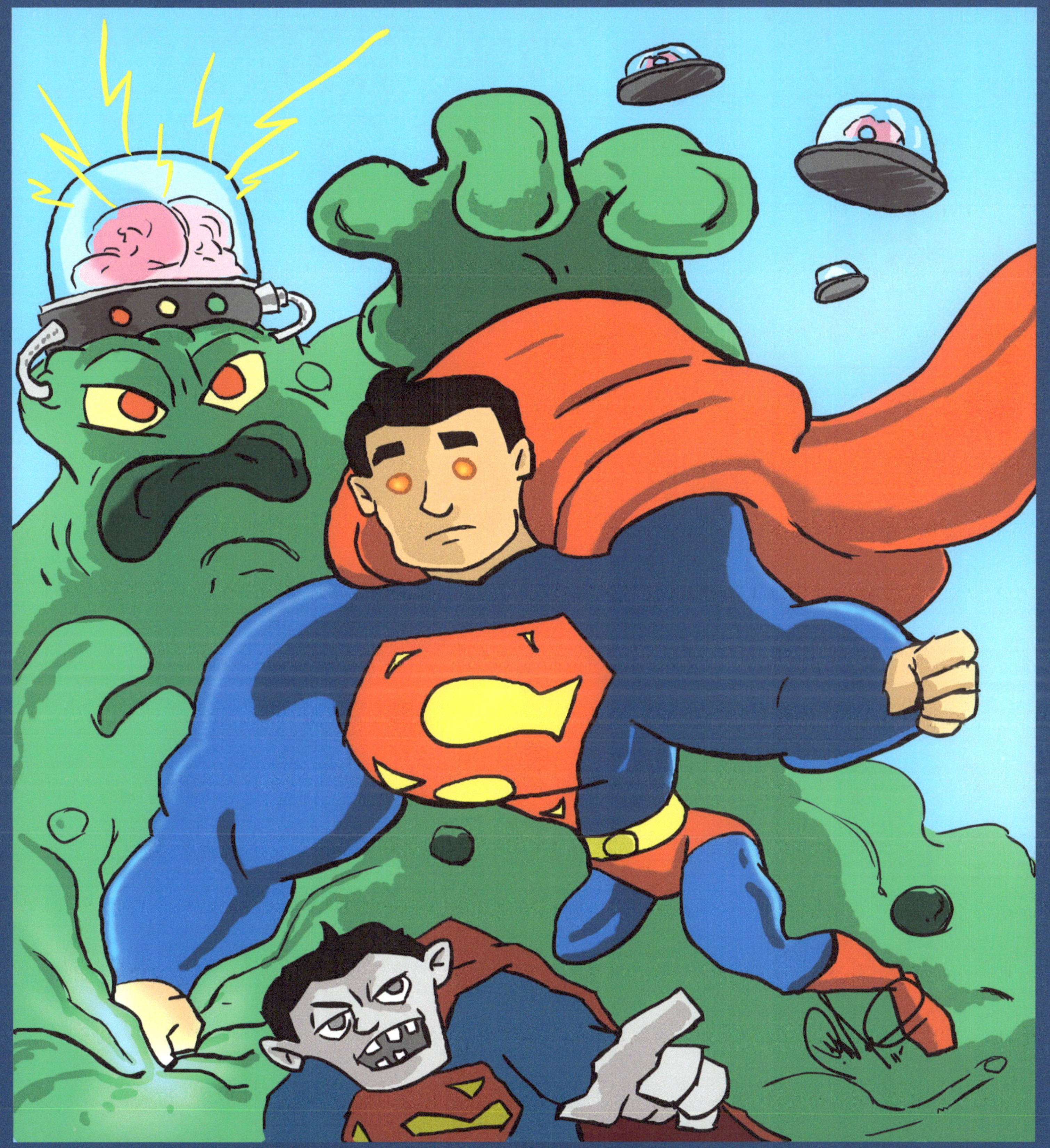
May all your days be
SUPER!

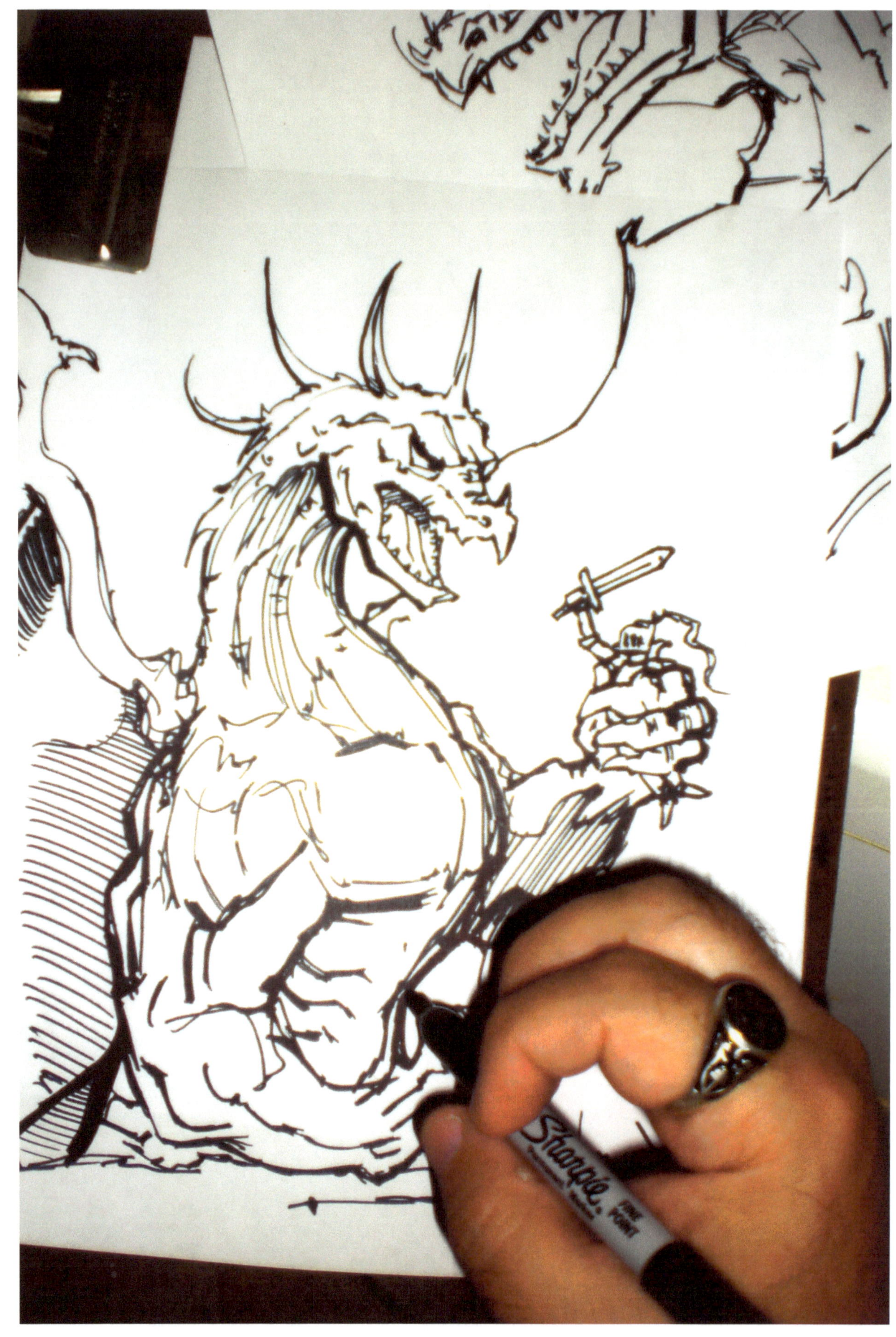

www.ingramcontent.com/pod-product-compliance
Lightning Source LLC
Chambersburg PA
CBHW042115030726
47599CB00002B/225